BEYOND THE OFFICE WINDOW

Discovery of Indian Ethos

BEYOND THE OFFICE WINDOW

Discovery of Indian Ethos

A.K. PANDE

KONARK PUBLISHERS PVT LTD

KONARK PUBLISHERS PVT LTD
206, First Floor, Peacock Lane,
Shahpur Jat, New Delhi-110049
Phone: (011) 41055065, 65254972, 22507103
e-mail: konarkpublishers@hotmail.com

ISBN 81-220-0788-0

Typeset by The Laser Printers, New Delhi, and printed at
ASK Advertising Aids Pvt Ltd, New Delhi.

This book is dedicated to my grand daughter Shreya and all other children like her, with the fond hope that as they grow, they discover and genuinely love the rich culture, tradition and heritage, in all its shapes and hues, which have helped to evolve that unique phenomenon called Indian ethos, and thus become good citizens not only of this country but of the world.

Preface

THERE is a touch of elegance in the way the armed forces keep their working and living environment. These stand out for their spruced up look, cleanliness and a right blend of nature and manmade. The Air Force Sports Complex, which is part of Safdarjang Airforce Station, at Safdarjang Road, New Delhi, is no exception. It is spread over a fairly large area, with lush green grounds and a variety of trees, shrubs and creepers. Flanked on three sides by grand sandstone and marble mausoleum of Safdarjung, the airport runway and the racecourse and the famous Jaipur Polo Ground respectively, it is, for its members and visitors alike, an enchanting place. For quite sometime, and till recently, a large board, fixed on one side of the elevated green of the 1st tee off, had a three dimensional and colourful picture of one of its tree-lined fairways. And at the bottom of the picture was a quotation from an unknown person. One could not miss a sense of pathos, though not intended, in those words in the context of the gallant fliers of the force. It read: "As you walk down the fairway of life, you must smell the roses, for you only get to play one round." And I loved it.

Engrossed as all are in their respective vocations, it is not surprising that most never look around as they walk down the 'fairway' and hence tend to miss the 'roses' altogether. And if the fairway be the vast subcontinent of India, one would then miss a rare spectacle of a myriad roses, with different and exotic smells, colours and shades. Calling India 'Kaleidoscopic' is an understatement, given the amazing variety of its culture, traditions, languages, creeds, literature, art music and historical monuments, in fact its entire heritage. And unlike the kaleidoscope, it has both, sharp and blurred lines. Its everchanging landscape across its length and breadth, gives it another dimension. Yet, despite its variety, an invisible silken thread, soft yet strong, binds it all unobtrusuively into a oneness. Some may call it "Indian ethos", which expression perhaps comes closest to define this phenomenon of oneness or this cohesive factor. Adi Shankaracharya, hailing from the southern extremity of the country, spreading his message of Gita and Upanishads, of Atman and Brahman to other extremities of the land, Ghalib, going to Benares and listening to the words of a sage there and writing that masterpiece in Persian 'Chirag-e dair (The Temple Lamp), Bade Ghulam Ali singing 'Hari Om tatsat' with a rare feeling, M.S. Subbulakshmi, the doyen of carnatic music, ardently admiring Bade Ghulam Ali Khan's Hindustani classical music, and singing Hindi Bhajans of Meerabai, in a voice and style which remain unmatched, Jesudas, singing Gita and hymns to Lord Ayyappa, and Bismillah Khan refusing to celebrate his 92nd birthday, which turned out to be his last, because terrorists had attacked 'his Benares', are some of the manifestations of this Indian ethos. It is a phenomenon which, while having elements of different religions, transcends to spirituality. And this phenomenon is better experienced than argued or explained. For this experience, one has to open his window, as it were, or move to the fairway, and look at what lies around and beyond. The scenario that unfolds, is simply mesmerizing, and out there every barrier crumbles, no one is different or a stranger, the unfamiliar becomes familiar, and one seems to belong every where.

With democracy having slowly but steadily taken firm roots in India, despite all odds, a new dimension has been added to Indian ethos. Nothing else would have suited the Indian ethos and genius better. We have still a long way to go with half the population still under poverty line besides subversion of the system by the powerful and perverted, and prevailing corruption. But things are changing. Many bright and honest people are now joining politics with a sense of service and mission, and choosing it to be their first "refuge"; the old adage, viz. "politics is the last refuge of a scoundrel" is fast losing its sting. With such people around, and the R.T.I., an independent judiciary and a vibrant and robust media in place, all bodes well for our democracy. I therefore thought it appropriate to include here the piece "The Mystique of the Ballot" which is based on my own limited experience of its working at the grassroots.

No profession provides a better opportunity to experience the Indian ethos and to be one with it, than the armed forces, paramilitary forces and the central civil services of the Union.

I consider myself to be privileged to have been a member of the central civil services. It meant serving in different parts of the country. I was further lucky to have a few assignments, which had all-India jurisdiction, and took me to numerous places all over the country. And never even once did I feel at any place in the country, that I was an outsider or a stranger. Some of the experiences of my official life as a public servant have been recorded by me in my earlier book *Grit That Defied Odds*. What I experienced outside my official life, or what I saw beyond the files or my office window, as it were, has been included selectively in the present book.

These experiences have come, not only from visits to different regions, the mountains, rivers, lakes and contrasting terrains of this land, but also from my acquaintance with some of the extraordinary personages, of past and present. For the personages of the present era, wealth of information is available in the visual and print media, and other sources. I had the good fortune of even meeting some of these living legends in person. And as for the great souls of the past, my limited knowledge comes from reading books of history—I was never a student of history—some biographies and sundry literature, not as a scholar, but as a curious onlooker, trying more to feel rather than understand the phenomenon called Indian ethos. In the process, some of these souls, left their lasting imprint on me.

Through these pages, I wish to share with others, some of my experiences, gained by the 'fairway', at a time when some elements, both from within and without, threaten to destroy not only the country's democratic and secular set up, but its very soul—the Indian ethos. Such elements must be defeated.

ANUP K. PANDE

Contents

CHAPTER 1

M.S., the Musician Saint

THERE are some events which etch themselves in one's memory and are perennial sources of some inexplicable joy and sense of fulfilment. The happenings of the morning of 20th February, 2002 is one such event for me. On this day, I had met Mrs. M.S. Subbulakshmi at her residence at Kotturpuram, Chennai. Very few events or meetings are as memorable and precious for me as those 45 minutes spent with her. Her benign presence cannot but leave an indelible impression on anyone. The meeting for me was a fulfilment of a desire which had lingered for three decades till it was fulfilled that day.

My first initiation into Carnatic music was through an audio cassette of "Silapathikaram" of MS in 1971 when I was posted as Assistant Collector of Customs at Nagapattinam. The cassettee was then lying with me for some time, and I played it casually for a change from Hindustani music, after I had returned from a strenuous coastal patrolling. The playing of the cassette proved a serendipity for me. The very first hearing of this piece cast a spell on me instantly, which has remained there ever since. This prompted me to acquire and hear her renderings of Meera's *Bhajans*, "*Vishnu Shahasranamam*" and so on. The appetite grew by what it fed on. Listening to her recordings opened up a whole new world of music for me, exposed as I was till then, only to Hindustani music. Since then I have listened to some of her musical pieces hundreds of times and had been having a desire to meet her in person.

I had some official work at Chennai in February 2002. I reached the city on 19th evening. A couple of days earlier, I had asked my colleagues in Chennai to request for a brief meeting with "MS". I was somewhat sceptical about her response, as I was told that since the demise of her husband, Shri Sadasivam—her friend, philosopher and guide for more

MS Subbulakshmi

than six decades—she had become more or less a recluse and had made very few public appearances. On landing at Chennai, to my delight and surprise, I was informed that she has consented to meet me at 10.30 am on 20th February at her residence located at 1st Main Road, Kotturpuram, Chennai. This was despite the fact that she had been indisposed for the previous three days. She had crossed 80 some years back.

My colleague, J. Sridharan, and I reached house No. 13, Kotturpuram sharp at 10.30 am. Shri Atmanathan, her Secretary and one more person, were waiting to receive us at the gate. Her house is a simple structure of modest size. The gate has two pillars, supporting the doors of iron grills. On top of one pillar on the left, word "Sivam" was engraved on a marble plaque, and on the pillar on the right, word "Subham" was engraved in an identical plaque. These are the abbreviated first names of Smt. Subbulakshmi and her husband. These two words aptly sum up her life and music too. While walking in, I could notice the still undisturbed kolam on the floor near the gate. After crossing the gate, we entered the short passage in the house which lead to a L shaped room with each wing of the size of about 15 × 10 ft. One wing of it was the drawing room, and the other was used for her 'riyaz'. A veena, mridangam and some other musical accompaniments were kept on the floor in this area. The house was spotlessly clean. The drawing room portion had a three–piece cane sofa set, with a middle table. 'MS' and Shri T.T. Vasu, a prominent figure in the cultural life of the city, and also a close friend of the family for over several decades, were already seated in the sofa. 'MS' was a picture of grace and simplicity. I greeted her with folded hands, and she responded with folded hands and a gentle smile. The impact of her personality, a perfect blend of simplicity, modesty and grace, was inescapable.

The drawing room, where we sat, had a spartan look. On the rack, images of Ganesh and a couple of other Gods, appeared to have been placed, not so much for decoration but as guardian and protecting deities of the house. The walls of the room, however, were replete with memorabilia consisting of photographs, spanning nearly seven decades of twentieth century, of great people like Mahatma Gandhi, U. Thant, Rajagopalachary, T.T. Krishnamachari and many others, whom the great lady had met during her illustrious career, and all of whom were her great admirers.

It took sometime for me to come to terms with the fact that I was face to face with a living legend. I kept on marvelling as to how a sonorous and lilting voice which has been gently finding its way into millions of hearts, falling "softer than petals from blown roses on the grass" and then lingering on and echoing endlessly, had been emnating from the frail frame of hers. She hardly seemed aware of the enormous impact of her music over millions of people spread over several generations.

The greetings over, we settled for some brief talk. She mostly spoke in Tamil, which was then translated either by Shri Vasu or by Shri Atman. She, however, followed everything that I spoke in English. She was polite to a fault and her face seemed to emit a unique radiance.

While we were conversing, some hot South Indian snacks and 'chutnies', were served in stainless steel plates. This was followed by coffee. "MS" was watching from the corner of her eye while my cup of coffee was filled from the pot and a spoon full of sugar was put in it, but was passed on to me without stirring. She, therefore, pointed out to the person who had passed on the coffee to me, that he had not stirred the sugar in my cup.

During the conversation I mentioned to her as to how I had first listened to her rendering of 'Silapathikaram' in 1971 at Nagapattinam and how I followed it up by listening to her Meera Bhajans in Hindi, *Vishnu Shahasranamam* and *Hanuman Chalisa* etc., and how I have listened to some of them hundreds of times since then. I also told her that her rendering which I like most is "Hari tum haro janan ki bheer". Her face lit up with a gentle smile on a mere mention of this Bhajan. And then she narrated what turned out to be a gem of an anecdote from her life, which she appeared to be cherishing immensely and which I guess, being one of the most precious of her jewels, she might have been displaying only on selected occasions. I was lucky.

What she narrated was something like this: During the forties, she had been invited to a function which Mahatma Gandhi was to attend, and his favourite bhajan "*Hari tum haro janan ki bheer*" was to be sung there. She was asked to sing it. However, she was diffident to sing it as she knew no Hindi and had not sung in Hindi till then, and thought that someone else could do it better. Mahatma Gandhi, no stranger to her voice by then, insisted that she alone should sing it, saying that even if she read it, it would be better than anyone else's singing. She was overwhelmed by the words of the great man and sang the song. How she sang it is now history.

"MS", in her voice, has been endowed with one of the greatest and priceless gifts from God. She has nurtured His gift with utmost care and in all humbleness and has used it not as something which is hers but His. And whatever she has achieved through it, she has been placing it back at the feat of God. The list of charitable concerts, which started from the inception of her singing career, seems to be unending.

Today we can only imagine how Meera might have sung her own bhajans 500 years back. What the posterity has inherited are her words in print. To me, and many would agree with me, if there is one voice which can truthfully render that divine frenzy of Meera's love and fathom the depths of those soul stirring thoughts, it is 'MS'. With the sophisticated audio technology now available, hopefully, MS's rendering of Meera can be heard by posterity 500 years hence, and more.

She received the highest award that the State can confer on an Indian citizen. However, she left behind even this lofty ground of the highest temporal honour and traversed to higher levels and received what cannot really be conferred by any individual, authority or institution. The award which came to her, in fact which had come repeatedly all through her life, was and is the instinctive outpouring of gratitude which has been emnating from the souls of millions of people around the world, cutting across cast, creed or language divide, who have listened to her divine voice time and again and have found immense bliss and pleasure in it and have benefitted from the numerous charities, associated with her. In the process, she had transited to a hallowed sphere of sainthood which admits very few great souls in each era, who are blessed by God.

The meeting over, I stood up to leave. I sought her permission to have a photograph with her. She readily agreed to this. After photographs, I again greeted her with folded hands. She stood up, slowly with some difficulty and effort, and responded with a *namaskar* and a smile.

Before leaving, her Secretary, Shri Atman, gave two gifts from her to me, a brochure of Music Academy, Chennai on her life, which she autographed on the spot for me, and two of her cassettes, brought out by HMV: 'Guru, Guha Pani".

Her countless renderings dedicated to God, over the decades, which had always sprung from her soul, seem to have permeated, over a period of time, her whole being and her face to me reflected that divine radiance, which I imagine, would have been there on Meera's face, as she trudged the dusty distances to the temples of Dwarka, Pushkar and Mathura with Ektara in her hands and bhajans on her lips.

"My morning was full of songs, let my sunset be full of colour". And the colour reflected in her face was that of divinity.

CHAPTER 2

"*Asi Gang ke Teer*"

I do not see myself as a religious person. A truly religious person, I believe, has certain positive traits, one may call them virtues, to none of which I can stake any rightful claim. Yet going to places like Haridwar, Varanasi, Tirupati, Amritsar, Velanganni, Nagoor or Nizamuddin, all of which I have visited more than once, have always given me an inexplicable pleasure and peace, a "calm of mind", where, "passions", though not "spent", at least get momentarily suspended or subdued. Life seems to come to a standstill in those moments and one is conveyed to a different world. One cannot explain why. Such impressions are beyond the realm of reason or logic. And these visits have, on occasions, been leaving a feeling of disquiet or unease too. A realization dawns, for a few fleeting moments though, how I am mostly engrossed, in my desires, gains, failures, frustrations and achievements which constantly work on the mind and how rarely I succeed, in wiping my mind of all these thoughts, even for a few moments, so as to get that magic stillness—a break for the relentlessly moving machine called mind. These visits have always meant a lot to me as they help to ward off the distracting thoughts and provide that stilness.

The joy is more intense for me, if the visit happens to be to Har Ki Paudi, Tirupati, Pondicheri, Varanasi or the Golden Temple. Listening to bhajans, or sabads or chanting of Sanskrit slokas from Gita or stotras have always enthralled me, because my mind is tuned to them since my childhood and they had been part of my milieu at that impressionable age. Though an early riser, I had been, on numerous occasions woken up even earlier, say, before 5 am, by the recitations from Ramcharit Manas or chanting of stotras by my mother—a daily and unfailing routine for her, or by the short but sharp blowing of the conch, marking the conclusion of her morning Pooja, before she plunged into endless chores associated with the bringing up of a large family single handedly, because my father was away on his vocation for a good part of a year accepting that the resources generated by it were perennially deficient to meet the needs of the family. And if she came out in one piece from that nerve racking experience, lasting close to two decades and withstood all odds, it was as much due to her indomitable will as the regular chanting of Ramcharit Manas, particularly Sunder Kand, Hanumanchalisa, some mantras and selected stotras. No wonder, such chantings and recitations continue to touch a familiar or emotional chord, in the inner recesses of my consciousness even today. I therefore do not see it as a sign of bigotry or rigidity, if chanting of Psalms or Koran or the call of muezzin, evoke similar response in some others for similar reasons. No one has choice of his birth.

Let me give a brief account of my last visit to Varanasi in January, 2005 as it was truly memorable. This was my sixth visit to that city, but it was not official. And I do not wish that it is my last. My first visit to Varanasi was sometime in 1967, when, as probationers in Customs and Central Excise Service of the Union, we were on our way to Govt. opium factory at Ghazipur, near Varanasi, as part of our training. Subsequent four visits to Varanasi were part of my official tours. After I retired from the service in 2002, I had a standing invitation from my brother-in-law Prabhat Joshi, who had been posted as a Colonel in the Gorkha Regimental Centre there around that time, to come for a few days and stay with them in the cantonment. The verdure and cleanliness of the cantonments have an irresistible charm. And then came another invitation in January, 2005 from Shri K.P. Mishra, a colleague, to attend his son's marriage in Allahabad. I responded to both together. After attending the marriage in Allahabad, my wife and I went to Varanasi where a warm welcome and hospitality were awaiting us, the latter remaining constant in warmth for five long days, rather a unusual feature for modern hospitality, which, with some exceptions has the tendency of tapering off with each passing day!

One is always at a loss for words to define the essence and character of this city. Yet such is the magic that the city weaves on its lovers, that each one, like me, finds it difficult to resist the temptation of defining the indefinable, or just wax eloquent about it, even if the results are some inane or platitudinous expressions. The city's character does not lie in its surface. For comprehending its true character and essence, one has to go beyond the surface and grope for its soul, which, in many ways is also the soul and ethos of India. There is nothing extraordinary about its surface and physical appearance, with the exception of Ganges, the sprawling ghats and the seemingly endless row of those beautiful buildings and temples along them which are a rare spectacle of divine beauty. Unlike Rome, Athens or Alexandria, it does not boast of any architectural wonders. One cannot see and feel its soul without first accepting its filth, narrow streets and milling crowds. In other words one has to see through this smoke screen to get at the real, the truely graceful face of the city. One only wonders how much more graceful it would be if there were no such smoke screen. Those who recoil at its first sight and refuse to go beyond it, get stuck with the first impressions and in all likelihood turn sceptics. For them, Varanasi is not different from any other ageing Indian city, lined with narrow and crowded streets, choked drains and dotted with heaps of garbage, with masses of people endlessly moving in and out of Vishwanath Temple and the ghats, where the pace of life has not changed for more than 2000 years. And they leave the city, wondering, how a tiny temple with a tinier deity, cast in rough hewn stone, installed inside it, embedded in the ground, a place accessible through an extremely narrow and over crowded lane, occupying an area no more than a few square meters, and which structure is dwarfed by the surrounding buildings and remains hidden till one almost reaches it, and whose interior can hold no more than dozen people at a time to have 'darshan', has drawn from time immemorial, millions of people, day after day, year after year without a break, from all parts of the country. They fail to see that this tiny structure is a symbol of faith passed down the generations. It is in this sense that it is not an ordinary city. It is a different city, different from all others and is only one of its kind in the world.

Varanasi, arguably the oldest living city on the earth, is associated not only with numerous temples, ghats and historical spots but also with great artists, poets, writers, craftsmen, musicians, saints, philosophers and freedom fighters. Some were born there.and some came from lands near and far. Its contribution to modern Hindi language is as unique and remarkable as is its sustenance of Sanskrit through ages.

Adi Shankaracharya, a prodigy and an ascetic, who had mastered Vedas, Upanishads, and all important scriptures, before he turned eleven, was advised by his guru Shri Govindpad to go to a city, none other than the ageless one, the city of Kasi, pay his obeisance to Lord Viswanath, and wait for his further commands. And young Shankara came to Kasi from the southern extremity of this land, set up an abode at Manikarnika ghat, paid obeisance to the Lord and meditated. He experienced the soul of the city and imbibed it. And then, inspired by the Lord and the ambience of the ageless city, he propounded the doctrine of 'Brahman' the only reality, becoming in the process 'Acharya', and then turned into a passionate missionary, destined to become the greatest in country's history, when he was barely twelve years old, and set out, in furtherance of his mission, first to the Himalayas, and thence to Mahismati, on the banks of Narmada, to have that spiritual debate, the most celebrated in Indian history, with Visvarup, popularly known as Mandan Misra. More debates and dialogues with other philosphers and thinkers of the age followed, and he moved on, in furtherance of his mission, to cover the length and breadth of the country, rather like a man in a hurry, understandable for one who was destined to live for only thirty two years, but long enough for the extraordinary man to complete his mission and leave an indelible imprint on history. He was a foster child of Kasi, spiritually speaking.

Since Shankara in the eighth century, not many might have soaked as deep in the mystique of the city or imbibed its soul, as Shehnai maestro Ustad Bismillah Khan. Khan Saheb, a devout Muslim, saw no conflict or contradiction, in playing Shehnai at the Balaji temple, in Varanasi. And he played it there lifelong. For him it meant 'Atman' reaching out to Brahman through the soulful tunes of his Shehnai. He apparently had little formal education and did not know English at all and he was candid about his lack of formal education. Some years back, during a felicitation ceremony for him at Siri Fort, Yehudi Menuhin, a lifelong friend and admirer of his, paid glowing tributes to his music. Khan Saheb who could make this out from the thunderous applause of the audience, responded thus in Hindi, with a touch of humour and in utter humility:

> "*Hum to 'likh lodhe hain, padh pathhar hain', inhone jo kuchh bhi kaha hoga, achha hi kaha hoga*"

The great man had used a popular idiom, replete with the fragrance of the soil, which does not yield easily to translation. It's free translation would be that he (Khan Saheb) is like an illiterate person, who writes one thing and reads it as something else; literally, it means one who reads 'Pathhar' though what is written is 'Lodhe' (Pebbles)—a fine distinction! He went on to add "(even though I have not followed what he has said, I know) he (Yehudi Menuhin) must have spoken only good about me." Such was the affection and esteem of the world famous violinist for the Ustad! And the Ustad was aware of it and acknowledged it in his own humble way, paying in the process his own tribute to the illustrious man. The geniuses have their own subtle ways!

Someone like him, gifted to communicate directly through his soul, is not hampered by language. The soul finds its own language. Even a gesture or even a monosyllable may communicate volumes. Nurtured by Varanasi, the Shenai maestro had imbibed something of the soul of the city. No wonder he had consistently refused to leave the city, despite prospects of greener pastures both within the country and abroad, because, as he confessed during one of his performances a couple of years before his death, in Kamani Auditorium, no other place has 'Ganga'! The terrorist attack on Sankatmochan temple and Varanasi railway station in 2004 had hurt the Ustad deeply. He could not accept that this could happen to his i.e., "Meri" Varanasi, a city beloved of god himself. He was an 'Indian Muslim', unique and different from any other, in the world. The incident made him so sad that he refused to celebrate his 91st birthday. Scores of people in the city and elsewhere were distressed by the Ustad's decision, though no one was surprised. And this proved to be his last birthday too, as he was not alive for his 92nd!

The Ustad had become one with the ethos of the eternal city, in fact that of India itself. One steeped in this ethos sees the country as one people and one humanity, where there are no dividing lines and fissures of religion, caste, region and language. And he was not alone in this. Many others had preceded him. And he was not the last either. He knew the soul of the land and the smell of its soil. The language he spoke had the hue and scent of its grass and its idiom sprung from its soil, as was the language and idiom of Khusro. Those who came only to invade, whether through Hindukush or the sea in the last two and half thousand years, and went away, could never know its soul or smell its soil and absorb its ethos that was born on its soil thousands of years ago and gradually evolved, absorbing the best of alien influences, as they kept coming through the centuries, from east, north, north-west, the sea and perhaps every direction. To sink in its ethos, one has to be born here, or live here long enough, with indulgence, not reluctance. And when Ustad spoke of Varanasi, there was the echo of eight preceding centuries in those words. He was echoing some of the greatest souls, an illustrious lineage of poets, saints, musicians and even some rulers, from thirteenth century onwards. All of them had spoken of universal love and brotherhood. And Varanasi and Ganga, came naturally to their mind. They were all quintessential Indian Muslims. Khusro was amongst the first in the illustrious line, dating back to the medieval ages. The fragrance of Indian soil was unmistakable, when he wrote "Na neend naina na ang chaina, Na aap aaven na bhejen patiyan". And for him nothing could symbolize love better than Ganga: "Khusro Ganga Prem kee, ulti waa kee dhaar; Jo paar hua so doob gaya, jo dooba so paar". Its translation would be: The Ganges of love has a different (opposite) flow: one who crosses it, is lost but one who gets drowned in it, gets salvation. This is the version sung by many a Quawwal, a version which seems to have come down by word of mouth through generations. Another version, however uses the word "Darya" instead of "Ganga". But "Ganga" rather than Persian 'Darya' goes better with native "Prem " and accomplished poet that he was, Khusro could not have been unaware of it. In fact he was a master of both Persian and Brij but never mixed one with the other. And Urdu would take another about five hundred years to evolve. This couplet, apart from having rare felicity and brevity of expression, has scent of Indian ethos in it, which could have come only from the quill of the Ameer. Six centuries later, there was the same unmistakable scent of Indian ethos in these inimitable words of Ghalib who tried to define temporal love, sans Ganga though: "Ishq per jor nahin, yeh wo atish hai Ghalib, Jo lagaye na lage, aur bujhaaye na bujhe" (Love is a firework, which cannot be kindled deliberately, and when kindled (of its own), is impossible to be extinguished.) But Ghalib's tryst with Ganga was to come elsewhere as mentioned later in these pages. These sentiments of two of the greatest poets of India, transcend age and the beauty of their home grown language is timeless. They have the hall-mark of great poetry and sublimity, which Mathew Arnold terms "high seriousness". And both are beyond translation. When Khusro's mentor and Guru, Nizamuddin Aulia, the Sufi saint died, Khusro expressed his profound grief, in these chaste words of Hindi, the language of the soil, which later on developed into 'Khari boli'–the precursor of present day Hindi: 'Gori soyi sez per, muh par daare kesh, chal Khusro ghar aapne, sanjh bhayee chahun des.' (……….. Khusro, go to your home now, as there is darknesss all around). The piece, written in the thirteenth century, is sung as a Quawwali till today, during the Urs of the saint every year.

Two centuries after Khusro came Kabir for whom God was one, and he spoke of him thus: "Sahib mera ek hai, duja kaha na jai, jo sahib duja kahoon, sahib khada resai" (I have only one God; if I say that there is more than one god, God becomes angry). And Kabir, who chided both Hindu and Muslim communities for their religious bigotry, because he loved both of them equally, is the only man in history whose body, as per the lore, was claimed by both the communities on his death, for performing his last rites. But what they found were flowers! Though this part of the lore may not withstand rational scrutiny but it truly reflects the affection and esteem of the people for the great poet. A hundred years later followed Emperor Akbar. The latter's even-handedness and love and reverence for all religions, being now part of history and folklore, needs no elaboration. Meerabai's fame as saint had spread far and wide in her life time itself. She was married into the royal family of Mewar, the most valiant and illustrious amongst the princely clans of Rajputana, who refused to accept the suzerainty of the mighty Mughals including Akbar, and whose valour occupies a pride of place in Indian history. That a princess so highly born, could renounce the royal palace of Mewar to become a 'Bairagan', much like the Himalayan prince before her, who renounced a kingdom two thousand years ago, was as much a miracle, as the legendary tales of valour of its kings and princes since the founding of the dynasty in the middle ages by Bappa Rawal in 734 A.D. Akbar, as per the anecdote, was so impressed by her devotion for Krishna, that he had a desire to have the darshan of this extraordinary soul at Brindavan, but incognito. And he did manage to get the darshan of Meera in the Krishna temple there. Meera, as per the lore, did come to Brindavan and spent quite sometime there. Agra is not far from Brindavan. Some credence can therefore be given to the story. However, even if this story is apocryphal, one rather would that such apocrypha, which has helped to generate love and understanding between communities, are left unprobed and undisturbed. Apocrypha, many times outgrows the truth, sometimes even wildly. But there has to be some element of truth for the wild growth to stem from. The emperor, one of the most tolerant and enlightened in country's and perhaps world history, despite lack of formal education, was after all the creater of Din-e-Elahi. The story fits with his image that has come down to us through generations. There must have been something in these great souls which gave rise to such apocrypha. Akbar's legacy, as that of the saints and poets, continued. His illustrious contemporaries like Abdurrahim Khan e-Khana, popularly known as Rahim and Malik Muhammad 'Jayasee' the poet with Sufi leanings and believer of one 'Nirgun Brahma' like Kabir and the author of Hindi epic 'Padmavat' too helped to keep the great tradition alive. Even in the twilight of the Mughal empire, the Nawab of Awadh, as commemorated in this gem of a bandish, was fond of playing Holi, with his subjects in Baradari:

"Holi khel rahen hain janabe Ali,
Ho mubarak manjari phoolon bharee,
Aisi holi khelen janabe Ali,
Baradari me rang bano hai
Sab mil khelen holi aisi"

The piece, possibly composed by legendary musician and Kathak dancer Bindadeen, has a timeless beauty. He had kept alive the tradition of Adarang and Sadarang, the court musicians of the Mughal Emperor Mohammad Shah 'Rangeele', perhaps the most illustrious musicians after Tansen and composers of many a bandish which are sung by classical musicians till today. The glorious cultural traditions of the Mughal court faded over the years. But they did not die out. They were reflected in the court of Awadh. And the reflection was as good as the original. The composite culture, art and music flourished in the inverse proportion to the political decadence of the period.

This bandish, sung in Bhairavi, still survives, not in Lucknow but in the remote hills of Almora, and continues to animate its evening Holi "baithaks", even today! In fact singers from small Muslim community of Almora participated in Holi Baithaks at Hindu homes till as late as three decades back. Sadly, this tradition has died out. But the nostalgia for the 'Rang' at Lucknow Baradari continues.

Then followed Ghalib, so aptly mentioned at the beginning and end of Shri Guha's highly readable history book, 'India after Gandhi'. Ghalib, according to Guha, on his way to Calcutta, had stopped at the city by the Ganges viz "Kashi" and spent some time there. He wrote a poem called 'Chirag-i-Dair' (Temple Lamps). The poet expressed his deep anguish at the conflict and privation of the era to a 'pristine seer' there and asked why "the doomsday had not come." To quote Shri Guha again, "Why does not the last trumpet sound?' asked Ghalib of the sage of Benares, 'who holds the reins of the final catastrophe?' This was the answer he got:

> The hoary old man of lucent ken
> Pointed towards Kashi and gently smiled.
> "The architect", he said, 'is fond of this edifice
> Because of which there is colour in life; He
> Would not like it to perish and fall'."

A century and half later Bismillah echoed Ghalib, but in different words and through a unique medium. There were some others like him in his own generation too. Bade Ghulam Ali Khan sang 'Hari Om tatsat 'with rare feeling. And the baton passed on by Khusro, after changing several illustrious hands through the centuries, did not stop with Bismillah. It has now passed on to a new generation, this time consisting even of theatre and film personalities. About two decades back, Amir Raza Hussain had charmed and mesmerized the Delhi cognoscenti by presenting the story of Ramayan in English, through a unique revolving theatre of large proportions at Chanakyapuri waste lands. It was a brilliant theatrical experiment, the like of which had not been seen before or since. But such performances have shelf life, roughly equal to the memory of the viewers. And after about two decades, the memory of that performance has all but faded. And Raza too is forgotten. But that scarcely matters. What matters is that a seven hundred years old tradition has survived the twists and turns of history. Indian ethos is alive. And the baton had been passed to future generations. It was perhaps lost upon most of the people that Raza was a link in the illustrious chain going back to Ameer Khusro. It is likely that some cynics might have frowned at his theatrical masterpiece as a gimmick, a populist and suspect act, meant to play upto the majority community or a simplistic or bizarre attempt at bridging the communal divide. But his attempt was an act of courage and vision. And Khusro and Ghalib would have nodded in approval. This is how the Indian ethos keeps itself alive.

The latest to receive the baton are Resul and Rahman, both musicians from south and from the film industry. They got Oscar for their music in 'Slumdog Millionaire' in 2009, a first for any Indian. Both gave the customary acceptance speech after receiving the awards. The stage available to them was famous and most coveted stage, befitting for a lineage going back to Khusro, Ghalib and Bismillah. The world was listening. A.R. Rahman, as is his wont, was forthright and brief. "I had a choice", he said with his disarming simplicity, "to love or to hate. I chose the former". Then followed Resul Pookutty. He was more forthcoming. He started by speaking about "home" (India), which, he said, was a land of 'Om', the word preceded and followed by (divine) silence And it meant a lot to him, he added. These words were not surprising from someone, who did his first 'katha prasangam' (performance of story recitation) at the Shiva temple in his village in Kerala. When asked a little later by someone from the media, what was his message for the people back home, he remembered that it was Shivaratri that day and he therefore wished them happy Shivaratri! These were the sentiments of two immensely gifted and sensitive souls nurtured by the eternal ethos of this ancient land. The stamp was unmistakable. Such words could have come only from Indian Muslim, someone nurtured in the ethos of this soil.

And yet there has been blood letting and brutal carnage between the communities for ages. Elements both within and outside never cease to stoke the fire of mutual hatred. They keep on doing it because many a time, they succeed too. One wonders if the supreme sacrifice of the Mahatma has been of any avail. Tranquillity of the society is shattered with an uncanny frequency, as vulnerable people on both sides spring from nowhere. And they would be satisfied with nothing less than 'an eye for an eye', no matter, to quote the Mahatma, if it "makes the whole world blind". And, unfortunate as it may sound, we may not have seen the last of the mayhem and carnage as yet. But had it not been for such souls on either side over the ages, the blood letting would have been even more frequent. That sanity ultimately prevails and the scars are erased and forgotten, rather slowly though, is to a great extent owing to such souls in the society. Communal harmony will continue to elude us unless each community is prepared to take a step or perhaps two, more than what it considers adequate or matching, to meet the other at half way mark, to give more than what it receives because what one considers more in these matters, is in fact just adequate. But when the occasion comes, each concedes only what, in its judgement is adequate, and blames the other for being unreasonable and not conceding enough. Against three steps required, each one takes, two, thinking that it has taken three. They need to take, what in their judgement are four steps! There is no other way to find a meeting ground. It is therefore not surprising that the meeting ground always eludes them. Those extra steps are always missing. But it must be conceded in fairness that quite a few Muslim saints, musicians and poets of India, have consistently faired better than others in the society, even if marginally, when it comes to taking those extra steps. They have been larger hearted. But taking the two main communities as a whole, there may not be much to choose between them, though things have been changing for the better, albeit slowly. In fact the smaller communities have shown greater understanding, some even adding a sweetness to the Indian ethos, like "sugar in milk". If some day in future, communal tensions, distrust and mayhem become a thing of the past and communal harmony becomes a way of life—which day is bound to come—some, if not substantial, credit for that, has to be given to such souls from all the communities, who, steeped as they were in Indian ethos, helped to sustain and keep it alive, through thick and thin. This however, is by way of a little digression.

Reverting to Varanasi, the images and names which come to mind instantly at the mention of the great city are Kashi Vishwanath Temple, the Ganges with its seemingly endless ghats and Goswamy Tulsidas. The first is the symbol of faith, hallowed by mythology and popularized by tradition; and the second, a phenomenon of nature, an inanimate object or just 'Ganga' for most of the highly educated, but for millions of others, through the ages, a living being with a soul, so revered that it is never mentioned without the suffix 'Ji' or 'Maiyya' (Mother), a river of Gods (Sur Sari), a gift of divinity to humanity, given in response to prayers of Bhagirath Muni, and conveyed to the Earth through the knotted and serpentine locks of Lord Shiva (Jata Shankari) to cushion the impact of its mighty fall from heaven into the Himalayas—so goes the legend. She has remained inseparable from both since then. Lord Shiva who protected the gods by swallowing the poison during Sagarmanthan, (churning of oceans) this time assumed a different role that of creator and not of destroyer, by facilitating the journey of the river from heaven to earth, and thus enabling the humanity to harness the river's life-giving force for its welfare. And the third, comparatively a recent phenomenon, was a living being, gifted with an extra ordinary mind and imagination, and a noble heart, who wrote an epic embellished with profound thoughts, delicacy of emotions and subtleness of sentiments, in a language which remains unsurpassed for its compactness, beauty and richness.

On reaching the city, I decided to go sight seeing in the forenoons. I covered Sarnath, Benares Hindu University and Ramnagar—the seat of old Kashi Naresh during the first two forenoons. On the third day, I went to Tulsi Ghat and the 'Kutia' of Goswami Tulsidas.

Goswami Tulsidas, who, as per common belief, was born in Banda, a town in eastern U.P., spent most of his life, at least most of his creative years, in Varanasi and breathed his last on the banks of Ganges. I have a vague recollection that, during my first visit to Varanasi in 1967, someone had mentioned to us that Goswami's Kutia (a small hut or cottage) was located on the banks of Asi river, just before it joins the Ganges, where, as per the lay, he lived and composed the epic 'Ram Charit Manas' and other works. The small river still had a narrow patch of open land all along its banks. That was a hurried visit and this is my only recollection of the place. I was therefore keen to visit the place again and have a closer and longer look at the area, particularly the place where Goswamiji lived and composed Manas.

My driver had some idea about its location somewhere near Tulsi Ghat on the Ganges. During our drive towards Tulsi Ghat, the driver explained to me that the name Varanasi has come from joining of two words, viz. Varuna and Asi which are names of two rivers which join the Ganges in the city. While we were about half a kilometer from the ghat, he pointed out to me a nullah or drain of dirty water about one and half to two meters in width, flowing towards the Ganges. There were houses on both sides of it, leaving no more than four or five meters of land on either side. This, he told, was once Asi river. It is only a question of time, before the narrow strip of vacant land on either side of nullah is also swallowed by new constructions. The driver however assured me that during the rainy season, the swollen drain does have the semblance of a small river. Varuna on the other hand which I had occasion to see the previous day on my way back from Ram Nagar, did still look like a small river with some open and unoccupied land on either side of it, which gave it the appearance of a bank of a natural river. The natural river water, if any, had however completely turned into grey by the larger volume of sewerage water in it. Within minutes we reached the place called Tulsi Ghat and the driver parked the car at a spot beyond which it could not go as the lane was too narrow. The place was at some height from the Ganges, and the Ghat, visible 30 meters down below, was accessible through several flights of steps separated by small platforms, with passages connecting them to Ashrams and Temples on either sides. I enquired about the Kutia of Shri Tulsidasji and someone pointed out to the entrance door of a building on the left, which I was told would lead to the 'Kutia', one floor down. The entrance gate led to a passage which was slightly dark. It was lunch time. No one was there. After going through a few rooms and a dark passage or two, and climbing down some steps, I reached a room, which had one window in front and a door on the side wall. The window was closed and the door was locked. There was a small door on its front side too which was also closed from inside. The small narrow balcony in front of the room faced the Ganges and commanded a panoramic view of the ghats, the opposite banks at some distance—the Ganges is very broad in Varanasi—the sands beyond and then the fields which

Goswamiji's Kutia by the Ganges (on the left)

stretched upto the horizon. The sight is spellbinding and the Ganges looks majestic here. My hunch was that this was the 'Kutia' or place of Goswamiji. And I was right. Goswamiii, being an ascetic, needed no more than that small and quiet space by the Ganges, enclosed by four walls, and having a window for light, air and a view of the Ganges. It is a modest structure. But it has been kept clean. Near the window, there is a marble plaque on the wall with the famous couplet inscribed on it—

> *"Samvat solah sau asi, asi gang ke teer*
> *Sravan shyama teej shani Tulsi tajyo sharir."*

This howevwr is slightly different from what we had learnt from our school text books as children, which was as follows:

> *"Samvat solah sau asi, asi gang ke teer*
> *Sravan shukla saptami, Tulsi tajyo sharir"*

Plaque, with the famous couplet on the wall of Kutia at Tulsighat

(In Samvat 1680, during Saptami of Shukla Paksha, in the month of Shravan, Tulsi relinquished his body on the banks of Asi-Ganges).

The inscription left no doubt that this was in fact the room or 'Kutia 'where the great man had breathed his last and also composed 'Ram Charit Manas' and other works. But there was no body at the spot to confirm it. I spent about 15 minutes near the room and its balcony and then went down the steps to Tulsi Ghat on the Ganges. It is perhaps the western most ghat on the Ganges. Here the river makes a deep, crescent like curve towards north which ends about 3-4 kms. away in the east. Most of the ghats of the Varanasi including Dashaswamedh, are located in this curve. Rising at a gradient from the platform of the ghats are numerous multistoried buildings, some of them architectural beauties, which make for the picture post card view of its ghats, so typical of Varanasi. From this spot, only the last one or two ghats at the other edge of the curve in the east are visible. I spent sometime there. On my way back I met someone from the place in the steps, who confirmed to me that the room with marble plaque and couplet inscribed on it was indeed the Kutia of Shri Tulsidas.

Accomplishing, what I missed last time, I went back to the greenery of Varanasi Cantt with a feeling of immense satisfaction.

I was somewhat saddened by the thought which crept in again and again, that one of the greatest sons of Varanasi has perhaps got a raw deal from posterity. Barring a few modern day elite and public school products, there may be very few from the vast populace of the Gangetic plains, and other Hindi speaking areas, living in the cities and the country side, who may not be able to recite at least a few lines from, 'Ram Charit Manas'. There may be very few even from the rest of the country, who may be unaware about the book. In terms of number of copies printed, few literary works in the world can equal or surpass 'Ram Charit Manas'. Perhaps, no literary work has gripped the imagination of such a large portion of humanity, illiterate, semi-literate and literate alike, for hundreds of years, as has this epic. No poetic work has been sung or recited or enacted as much, in houses temples and public places, as the case may be, as 'Ram Charit Manas'. There is hardly any great Indian classical singer, irrespective of his creed who has not sung some of the Bhajans of Tulsidas. Yet all that remains by way of a memorial to him is that small 'Kutia' at Tulsighat. Asi is gone. Its banks have shrunk. The poet himself, who needed just a small room with a window for fresh air, light to read and write, and a view of the Ganges for inspiration, lived at a different level, scarcely concerned about any manifestation of adulation or tribute. His admirers can perhaps take comfort from the thought that for someone like him, who lives in the minds of the people, a monument or a commemorative structure is of little significance. However, if a structure or a place closely associated with his life or his memory is already there, it should not be allowed to decay and disappear but cared for and protected for posterity. The people of Varanasi were perhaps helpless against the inexorable march of time, the

View of Shakespeare's house at Stratford-on-Avon

phenomenon of urbanization and population explosion, which sweep everything before them. Varuna and Asi are no exception. This march of time can be slowed and even almost checked, as has been proved my many European countries, by harnessing science and technology and by careful planning. As a proof, one has to see Stratford-on-Avon, the birth place of Shakespeare. His house there has been preserved in its original shape, with even some of the utensils, linen and furniture intact. The city with its clean roads, streets and theaters and the Avon river with white ducks swimming in its dark but clean water, perhaps looks more beautiful than it might have been at any time in the past. Excepting the 'Dark Lady Of The Sonnets" which still remains a mystery, thanks to the tireless research through the ages, vital facts about Shakespeare's life and times are now known. Even his Globe theatre has been recently recreated at the same spot by the Thames, as true to the original as possible, and this time more lasting. Those people are passionate about their heritage. However, Shakespeare's illustrious contemporary by the Asi river, has been less blessed. Barring the places of his birth and death, other details of his life are shrouded in mystery and where such details are available, they are scanty and riddled with controversy. It may be too late to restore Varuna and Asi to their original glory. It might have been possible 50 years back. It must however be said in fairness to the people of Varanasi that for a poet so dear to their hearts, they have paid fitting tribute by constructing Manas Mandir, a beautiful structure of ample proportions, slightly removed from the Ganges, with entire Ram Charit Manas inscribed on its walls.

Nearby Sarnath, in comparison, has fared better, as it still retains its pristine and rural charm. Even today, one has to cross vast expanse of open country side for a few kilometers to reach it. They have to be kept, as it were, frozen in their present state, so that Sarnath continues to breath in future too.

Sooner or later, Varuna will degenerate into a large city-drain, an integral part of city's sewerage system, unadulterated by natural river water! Prospects of restoring it to its original glory look remote. It is therefore time that the city's name 'Varanasi' is now changed to Kashi which is its ancient name. If this is done then, as and when Varuna's transformation into a city drain is complete, the metamorphosis would go unnoticed because the river would no more be associated with the name of the great city!

CHAPTER 3

Babur's Memoirs and the Mystery of Ram Mandir

IT had been simmering for a couple of decades. It developed into some sort of frenzy in the late eighties which reached its crescendo in 1992. Then came the bang. The leading newspapers around the world carried the headlines about the demolition of Babri Masjid. It even made the cover story of 'TIME'. Then followed the communal mayhem and the trauma of Mumbai blasts. The issue is far from dead and the Ram Mandir—Babri Masjid imbroglio remains unresolved, though a bit subdued for sometime now. One only wishes that it does not come to a boil again.

For me Mumbai blast brings back some of the most painful memories of my official career. The investigations conducted by Mumbai police and C.B.I. had indicated certain acts of omissions and commissions on the part of some police and customs officers of Raigarh, south of Mumbai, which had helped the perpetrators of the blasts, all important members of Mumbai underworld like Tiger Memon and Dosa, to successfully smuggle explosives from Dubai into Raigarh coast and later use them in these blasts. These officers had double crossed the nation by agreeing to connive in the smuggling of silver for a consideration, and they in turn were double-crossed by the smugglers, who smuggled explosives, not a part of the deal, along with silver. While these half a dozen officers along with some police officers were detained under POTA by the Maharashtra Govt. the task of initiating the proposals for the dismissal of the customs officers from service under Article 311 of the Constitution, in the interest of the security of state, fell in my lap as Chief Vigilance Officer of the department. Though justified by the circumstances and required by law, it was one of the most painful tasks of my career.

Since the Babri-Rammandir issue had assumed or was made to assume such political and communal dimensions, and dominated the psyche of the vast number of Indians in recent years and was the direct cause of Mumbai blasts, which, as mentioned, had an unpleasant and painful association for me, I was curious to know, if in fact Ram mandir was demolished by Babur as is believed by many in the majority community, and whether Babri Masjid was constructed over it. In my judgement, no source could be more authentic to throw light on this issue, than Baburnama, the memoirs of 'Padishah' Babur. I was aware that, for someone like me, with scrappy knowledge of history and archaeology and with just one source i.e the memoirs to draw upon, it may not be easy to unravel this skein, in which effort, men with much better credentials and far superior knowledge are yet to succeed. And I did fail, as the memoirs provided no answer to my questions. But I was delighted by some of the discoveries I made about Babur from my reading of the translation of the memoirs by Annette Susannah Beveridge, which I borrowed from the small library of the Department of Revenue. And surprisingly, Babur emerged as an extraordinary man from the memoirs, quite different from the commonly held perceptions about him.

In the entire memoirs, I could not find any mention about demolition of Ram Mandir or construction of Babri Masjid anywhere. It is unlikely that a fastidious and honest writer of chronicle like him could have missed on this important event, when, he in fact recorded many others of lesser import. It is more likely that the demolition of Ramjanmabhoomi Mandir in Ayodhya, if it really existed, was the work of some overzealous general of Babur, sent on expedition to that region. The only entry in the memoirs, rendering Babur vulnerable to the charge of iconoclasm, was of 28.9.1528 when Babur was in Gwalior. It reads:

"We saw the imarat called Badal-gar which is part of Man Singh's fort; went through the Hatipul and across the fort to a place called Urwa—3 sides of Urwa are solid rock. On these people have cut idol statues large and small, one large statue on the south side being perhaps 20 qari high. These idols are shewn quite naked without covering for the priveties. Urwa, is not a bad place; it is shut in; the idols are its defects: I for my part ordered them destroyed."

By calling the 'naked' idols as the 'defects' of the place, not apparently approximating to his own concept of art and architecture, and a keen builder himself, he was perhaps expressing the disapproval of either a cognoscenti of both, or of a puritan and a devout follower of his religion, whose tastes and beliefs were shaped, as is mostly the case, by his upbringing, milieu and time.

The very next entry for the same date leaves one in no doubt that the the demolition of those idols was not the result of a Taliban like frenzy, or of uncontrollable rage of a bigot or iconoclast, but the result of an instinctive reaction of person in whose concept of art and architecture the naked figures did not quite fit in. Otherwise the bigot and icoconoclast in him would not have spared some other idols in the same area. Idols per se did not seem to offend his sensitivities, and he left those, that were not "naked ", intact:

"We rode from the flower-garden to visit the idol houses of Gwalior. Some are two and three stories high, each story rather low in the ancient fashion. On the stone plinths are sculptured images. Some idol houses, college-fashion, have a portico, large high cupolas and madrasa like cells each topped by a slender stone cupola. The lower cells are idols carved in the rock.

After enjoying the sight of these buildings we left the fort by the South Gate."

Babur in fact saw these idols and architecture with a connoisseur's eye, not missing even minor details and enjoyed their beauty and then left them untouched. Only a genuine lover of artistic beauty, and not an iconoclast would have behaved in that fashion. In fact one can see the Sahastra Bahu temple in Gwalior fort (Babur may be referring to it as "idol house") which the local people also call Sas-Bahu temple and the carvings on the rock-faces of the fort, near the elephant gate, intact even today. He was different from many of his predecessors in Delhi Sultanate. And he did not do even in the medieval ages, though Bamiyan was part of his empire, what the vandals and compulsive iconoclasts did there in the twenty-first century—destroy those massive and beautiful Buddha images carved out of rock face, with flowing robes in stone, in the celebrated Hellenic style of Gandhar, also known as Bamiyan Buddhas. They belonged not only to them but to the entire humanity. They therefore robbed the entire humanity of a priceless treasure. They have disappeared from the face of the earth, and cannot be retrieved! It did not matter to them that their own forebears, had looked at them in admiration and awe and left them untouched for more than two thousand years. It cannot be said about someone like Babur, who enjoyed 'the sight of these buildings' at Gwalior, which had 'idols carved in the rock', that idolatry was anathema to him, as it was to many others in that age, and to many even today. But to understand his mind and be fair to him, one has to don the glasses of that age and not the modern ones, which would definitely tend to distort the picture. He was the product of his time, who could not shake off its shackles and transcend it, as his illustrious grandson did. Very few in human history have done that, because it calls for true greatness. If anyone of his age had that potential and promise, it was he, richly endowed as he was by an exceptional mind and many sterling qualities of heart. But in his case, matters were compounded by the fact that he was a man in a hurry, eager, after his several expeditions of 'Hindustan' to revert to the cool hills of Kabul, and was granted only forty-six years of life. His is therefore one of those rare cases of history, who was destined for true greatness but sadly missed it by a whisker.

This was not all that I discovered. This man certainly was anything but a monster. The memoirs clearly mirror a man of parts, a man who was one of the most erudite of his time, a poet, a great lover and connoisseur of art and music, a sportsman and a keen observer of nature—one who would not miss the distinct colour patterns even of a tiny bird or the difference in the flavour of similar fruit from different regions; a man who would keep his word at any cost and one who would never forget a good turn done to him. And when it came to the battle-field, he was a fierce enemy who would order, as a matter of strategy, to raise a 'pillor of heads' in the realm of the vanquished, whether he be a Muslim or Hindu King. He was a great general and born leader who was proud of his Timurid ancestry. He was exceptional, who could wield the sword and the quill with equal perfection. Particularly delightful was the discovery of this entry of the year 1519 in the memoirs, made when he was yet to embark on his several expeditions to 'Hindustan'.

"I had never been to Rustam-maidan road. I went with a few men to see it. ... To the South is a smallish spring. ... This is a narrower dale, but still there is a plot of green meadow below the smaller trees ... the little dale is charming.

From the summit of the range, looking South, the Karmash and Bangash mountains are seen at one's feet; and beyond the Karmash show pile upon pile of rain clouds of Hindustan. Towards those other lands, where no rain falls, not a cloud is seen."

"Pile upon pile of rain clouds of Hindustan'! This was perhaps Babur's first glimpse of distant Hindustan. 'Pile upon pile'—no other three words could have better described the dense clouds of Indian monsoon.

This was a view of the endless plains of Hindustan from the North-Eastern heights of Hindukush. And perhaps there is a hint from Babur, the man who knew nature by instinct, what these clouds meant to the plains of India, scorched by several months of torrid summer. The arid or desert lands have no clouds: "where no rain falls not a cloud is seen". He could possibly be referring to Baluchistan and nearby areas.

For teeming masses of humanity in India, for whom the sun relentlessly pours fire during the long summer, and where failure of monsoon means famine, drought and death, the first showers of monsoon are indeed a promise of new life, each drop a 'Swati Nakhshatra, ' maturing into grains of food, more precious than pearls. The sound of the first showers of monsoon is a divine music to Indian ears. No wonder, therefore, raga Malhar is perhaps one of the most beautiful of the Indian ragas. It echos and mirrors its life. It is born out of nature. And therefore it's 'music' and 'soft voices' never die but linger on and on.

Babur was neither the first nor the last to come under the spell of "rain clouds of Hindustan". The monsoon clouds and the rain have been casting their spell on one and all through the ages. And this includes the greatest amongst the Sanskrit poets—Kalidasa—who, more than a thousand years before Babur, wrote 'Meghdoot', and captured the timeless beauty of clouds and the rainy season in his inimitable language. The very second stanza of 'Meghdoot' gives an idea of this. It reads:

> "*Ashadhasya prathamadivase meghamashilastsanum vaprakridaparinatgajaprakshaniyam dadarsha*"

(on the first day of Ashadh he (Yaksha) saw that the mountain top, covered by the clouds was looking as if some elephant was playfully trying to fell mound of earth with its head.)

And then there was Tansen, the musician in the court of Babur's illustrious grandson—one of his Navratnas, the most revered name in Hindustani classical music, who captured the beauty and magic of 'clouds of Hindustan' and the rains, the very essence of the elements, not in words, but in 'swara', in a raga, rightly named after him, 'Mian Ki Malhar'.

Both, the Sanskrit poet of old and the great musician of the Mughal era were rendering an immortal paean to a timeless and beautiful phenomenon of nature.

In Babur's reign, Afganistan was the core of his empire, with Hindustan forming its eastern extremity, in contrast to the later Mughal era, commencing from Akbar, when Gangetic plain was the centre of the vast empire, of which Afganistan formed the western extremity. Babur's stay in India was no more than an extended expedition. He was unfamiliar even with the idiom of this land. He sought the aid of translators to confer with the local princes and populace. And he died a premature death. Had he been born in India like Akbar or if he had stayed in India longer, it is more than likely that, under the patronage and inspiration of a man so richly endowed by nature, some music prodigy, may be a Haridas, who, as per the apocrypha, was Guru of both Tansen and Baiju Bawra, would also have composed, like his celebrated disciple, some immortal Raga for the posterity! His sensitive and intelligent mind could not have missed the mystique of Vedant or Sufism nor the fact that some of the oldest religions of the world have co-existed here for centuries, without creating any ripples but instead, each contributing to shape its unique ethos.

My earlier impression of Babur as a ruler, formed on the

basis of my skimpy knowledge of history and the school text books, was not much different from what I had of many other rulers of the medieval ages. Reading of his memoirs changed it all. He stood apart from all others of his age. It is a pity that a man so profusely gifted by providence could not live up to his full potential and rise above his age, as did Asoka before him and Akbar after him. If only he had spared those idols of Urwa!

If he had been born and brought up here, or lived here longer, and breathed the air or smelled the earth of 'Hindustan', his sensitive soul could not have been any less mesmerized, that than of Amir Khusro's, three centuries before him, by the magic of such native idiom as 'Bahut Kathin Hai Dagar Panghat Ki' or 'Sakal Ban Phool Rahi Sarson' and whose mastery over Brij bhasa was comparable to his mastery of Persian. And who knows, he would have even seen a different beauty in the people of Hindustan, whom he did not find beautiful during his forays!

And lest one errs like numerous others in the past, and Babur was one of them, one has to remember that to comprehend the soul of India, one has to live in and feel India, long enough to see through its dust, heat, poverty, sloth and mind boggling contradictions. India grows on everyone rather slowly. But Babur was a man in a hurry.

The reading of memoirs led to one more realisation. Like many others, I had been viewing the medieval times and its people through modern glasses. This, as I realize now, gave a distorted and rather misleading picture. The result would be no different, if someone were to view the modern times with medieval glasses. People of each age, kings and emperers not excepted, are products of their times and milieu. But history, once in a way, throws up some rare exceptions, who rise above their times and for that reason therefore belong to no particular time or age and they look always the same, no matter through which glasses one sees them.

CHAPTER 4

The Mystique of the Ballot

WHILE posted as Additional Director General in the Hqrs. of the Directorate of Revenue Intelligence, I had been planning, right from early 1991, to visit its regional office at Lucknow. I had to postpone it several times because of other pre-occupations in Delhi. I finally, fixed the visit for May and decided to cover nearby Kanpur as well. As my children were having summer vacation by this time, they also wanted to go along. I therefore cancelled my air ticket and instead booked seats by Shatabdi Express to Lucknow for the entire family.

I have nostalgic memories of Lucknow as I had studied in Lucknow University. I still have a few friends and relations there. And Lucknow is one of the few cities where the old world charm still lingers. And one fine morning at the end of May, as we set out for the railway station at 5 am, we were greeted by a waft of cool air and there was no hint of the scorching heat of the day that was to follow. It was indeed a pleasure to travel by Shatabdi Express, a new experiment then, as the train had only one stop and it departed on the dot and reached the destination in time. It was altogether a new experience of train travel at that time. The next two days were spent in attending to my office work during the day time and visiting some monuments and meeting friends and relations during the spare time in the mornings and evenings. I was really relishing the smug feeling of leaving behind the hectic and tense life of Delhi and of being out of its reach. We moved to Kanpur on the third day. I had a few official engagements there. No sooner had I reached the residence of my brother-in-law Subhash Joshi, (he was posted as Senior Superintendent of Police there), than his duty office informed me that there was a message for me from the "Chief Electoral Officer" of U.P., from Lucknow, that I should contact him immediately. I was taken by surprise and could not figure out as to how the Chief Electoral Officer of U.P. could be so much concerned about a prospective voter, and that too from beyond his jurisdiction! Before I could contact him, a written message was received at the Police Control Room at Kanpur that I had been appointed as one of the Central Observers in Assam for the forthcoming elections and I should proceed to that place immediately. While I was collecting myself, a sepoy from the Office of Collector of Central Excise and Customs at Kanpur came in and delivered a note from the Collector. The note in fact was the text of the message from my Hqrs. in Delhi which had in turn received it from the Election Commission. Everything now fell into place. I had been appointed Central Observer for three Assembly Constituencies in Udalguri Sub-Division in Mangaldoi Parliamentary constituency in Assam for the Assembly and Parliamentary elections due on 8.6.1991. Darrang District of Assam covered the Mangaldoi Parliamentary Constituency. I did not till then know what were the precise duties and responsibilities of the Central Observer though I had some vague idea about it. I was required to reach Udalguri before 7th June, 1991 and visit the area to satisfy myself that all the arrangements for polling had been made. It was already 5th of June. I was a bit disappointed to see my original plan going awry. It was difficult to make a booking by air at such short notice and the train journey was out of question, because of the time and distance involved. I did not even know the exact location of Udalguri in Assam. I therefore requested my colleague in the Hqrs. at Delhi to ascertain from the Election Commission, if I could be excused from this duty, because of paucity of time. I did not hear anything on 5th. However, on the 6th of June, I got a message that my request was placed before the Chief Election Commissioner Shri Seshan and he had directed that I must go and tour the area before the polling day. I came to know later that action was taken against some officers who failed to report for duty assigned by Election Commission. Election Commission could not be taken lightly by anyone anymore.

I could not but marvel at the precision and speed with which I was tracked down. This was the proof of a single minded pursuit of purpose and of the determination of the man, who controlled and directed the electoral machinery with an efficacy never witnessed before, and of which I got the feel from the terse electronic communication received at Kanpur. I had thus got a brief introduction of the man behind the message without even seeing and meeting him. He had set the gigantic election machine in motion at such a short notice. It was for the first time in its history that Election Commission had made its presence felt so strongly. Shri Seshan gave hint of the shape of the things to come when, in one of the interviews in the T.V., and in response to a question, he answered with those memorable words "I will bark, and if they still don't listen, I will bite". "They" meant the establishment, prospective candidates and political parties. His bark was bad and his bite, worse. Shri Seshan had arrived. Coming, as these strong words did, from an constitutional authority, they could not be ignored by anyone. The presence of Election Commission became assertive and unmistakable and the people for the first time got the definite impression that the Election Commission was an independent creature of the Constitution, and not an adjunct of the Executive. The only other time when the presence of the Election Commission was felt strongly, though not as much, was during the general election immediately after lifting Emergency in 1977, when posters appeared on the roads and streets of Delhi, urging people to vote without fear, as their ballot was secret. What the posters said was axiomatic, but at that point of time, just after lifting of the Emergency, those words seemed to convey a bold and profound message. I presume, similar posters must have appeared all over the country. And vote people did, and in large numbers too. And their vote this time changed the course of Indian politics forever. And this time around, during Shri Seshan's tenure, the unprecedented step of appointing, amongst others, the Revenue Services Officers of the Central Government, as Central Observers, was taken. This was a new concept. The Central Government Officers owed no allegiance to any State Government. The Election Commission could thus have a direct and independent feed back regarding the conduct of polls from every part of the country. Only officers of the rank of Joint Secretary were assigned this duty by the Commission. Later on, when the election expenses of the candidates and political parties assumed importance because of the ongoing intense public debate on this and several other issues related to the elections, the concept of Expenditure Observer was introduced. This measure, it seems, has proved quite effective, though it may not be fool proof as yet to check excessive and unaccounted expenditure. When the concept of the Expenditure Observers was first introduced, the Revenue Services officers were appointed as Expenditure Observers. As large numbers of such observers were required during election, both, the officers of the rank of Directors and Joint Secretaries were appointed as Expenditure Observers. This practice is still continuing. However, when I was appointed

Central Observer, the concept of Expenditure Observer was yet to evolve; therefore we were sent as General Observers, which duty was earlier assigned to the State and All India Services Officers alone.

As I set about making arrangements for my journey, to my pleasant surprise, I found that the Railways and Airlines had already been sounded by the Election Commission about the movement of the Observers and other officers on election duty. I was therefore able to secure a seat in the Shatabdi Express up to Delhi without difficulty even at such short notice and left that evening itself, leaving behind my family. I reached Delhi at 11.00 p.m. on 6th June 1991. An officer from my office had come to the station and gave me a set of detailed instructions received from the Election Commission along with my air ticket upto Guwahati and back, which the officer had arranged as per my instructions. I took the 6 am. flight to Guwahati the next day i.e. 7th June, 1991. I glanced through the important instructions of the Commission during the flight. The heavier reading of the 'HAND BOOK FOR RETURNING OFFICERS' was taken up in the night on reaching the destination. I was thus clear about what lay ahead. In fact I was quite excited about the election duty which I was performing for the first time. The journey to Assam proved quite an interesting experience. I now realize in retrospect, as to what I would have missed if my request to opt out of this duty had been acceded to. During the flight to Guwahati, in between the study of Election Commission's instructions, I kept on peeping outside the window and enjoyed the sight of ever-changing Gangetic landscape below and the Himalayan ranges on the left, enveloped in clouds, every now and then.

When our plane landed at Guwahati we were received and taken to the the airport lounge. There I met several other Observers who had arrived from other parts of the country for the same duty in the state. We were given a warm reception by the staff of the State Election Department. Perfect arrangements for our movement and stay had been made by the State authorities. After having a cup of tea at the Airport lounge, we set out for our respective destinations in separate vehicles. I was accompanied in the car by an official of the Forest Department of Mangaldoi and a posse of armed security personnel from B.S.F. followed in a jeep. This precaution had perhaps been taken in view of the looming threats from ULFA and BODO activists in the area, though we were given to understand that both had given their word not to disrupt the process of the elections. Indeed, the whole of Darrang District and particularly, Panery, Udalguri and Mazbat constituencies—the areas of my duty, were reported to be the stronghold of BODO movement. And some element of fear still seemed to permeate the air. Only a month back, a Circle Officer of police in that area had been shot dead by Bodo militants. I had been cautioned that the whole area was sensitive. The security personnel always accompanied me during my entire stay whenever I moved out of the Circuit House to the place of duty. But what I experienced in the next two days, was unique. Whereever I went, I got the unmistakable impression that the presence of the Central Observer was noticed and felt. And at the back of my mind there was a constant feeling that I was the extended arm of the Election Commission and therefore I could weather any untoward, difficult or slippery situation, and could not be cowed down or influenced in any manner. Neither I nor the other observers deputed by the Commission had any stake in the state. The powerful impulses emitted by an Election Commission, which seemed to have rediscovered itself, were felt even in the remotest corners of the country. I realized how important the institution of Election commission was, for free and fair elections and consequently the survival of democracy in the country.

After leaving the Airport, we passed through the outskirts of Guwahati city and followed the Guwahati—Tejpur road. Within minutes we crossed the Brahmaputra river. This was my first glimpse of the mighty river. Rain had turned its waters muddy, and it was full of floating islands of water-hyacinth with birds perched on some of them or hovering around them. The river was so wide that its opposite bank seemed to merge with the horizon. I had not seen a river of this dimension before. There could not have been a better initiation to the State of Assam than the view of Brahmaputra, 'Lohit' for the local people. Within hours of leaving Delhi, I found myself in the heart of Assam. The road which was tolerably good, meandered through the green paddy fields, dotted every now and then with cluster of trees. The famed forests of Assam, however, were nowhere to be seen though the sight of tea gardens was quite common. But it was still one of the greenest landscapes that I had seen.

I reached Mangaldoi circuit House during lunch time. Some district officials headed by a young lady ACS (Assam Civil Service], Officer were present to receive the Observers including me. We were given a warm reception, which was followed by a briefing. After taking lunch and resting a while I set out for Udalguri, which was to be my Hqrs. for the next few days and again during the counting of votes from 16th of June onwards. Other Observers went to their respective destinations. Udalguri, the sub-divisional Hqrs., covered the Assembly constituencies of Paneri, Mazbat and Udalguri. It is about 2-1/2 hours drive from Mangaldoi. The area of Udalguri commenced from Panery which is about half way from Mangaldoi. With canvassing over a day earlier, a calm had descended on the scene. I could, however, notice prominent writings on the roads and the walls of the houses and party flags fluttering in every locality. The electioneering, it appeared, had been quite vigorous. I could also notice that what the area had missed by way of industrialization, had been more than atoned for by an ambience, totally unspoiled by pollution. It was a vast canvas of green paddy fields with leit-motif of sheets of water and cluster of trees of different varieties. To breathe a air so pure and, pristine, unpolluted since time immemorable, was a unique feeling. In fact this pristine air seems to permeate the whole of north-east. One only wishes that the future economic development that may, in fact, must, take place, is not at the cost of its environment.

The road to Udalguri was narrow and the traffic was moderate. The earth on both sides of the road had a carpet of green grass which terminated where the tar of the road began. The road in fact looked like an over sized black ribbon with broad green border on either side. To my left, I could see the Bhutan hills at a distance, partially covered by monsoon clouds. The northern border of Udalguri is contiguous to Bhutan border all along. By the time I reached Udalguri late in the evening, I had crossed numerous rivers and streams emanating from the Bhutan hills and rushing, as if in a hurry, to deposit their precious cargo –the crystal clear water, into the ocean. The road-bridges over most of the streams were made of wood. On a few occasions, I could not resist the temptation to pause and stand by the side of these streams and have a closer look at the pebbles in the river-bed and the flora nearby. But I had constraint of time. The task at hand was the first priority, and I had to make the best of about three hours left, before it was dark. Primed as I was, with fresh knowledge of polling process, acquired rather hurriedly, I went around, visiting as many polling stations as possible to satisfy myself that the arrangements made were satisfactory. This took me to numerous schools and public offices in the country-side, which were notified as polling stations. Whether the buildings were new or ramshackle, there was nothing wanting in the arrangements made. I had in the past seen the polling stations in Delhi and other big cities, all of which were easily accessible. This was for the first time that I was seeing so many polling stations, which could be approached only by a country-path passing through paddy fields or stations located in the solitary buildings, surrounded by the fields, with clear water channel running parallel to the country-path leading upto them. My visits to all polling stations were unannounced and by surprise. Yet, I found the polling officers and the security staff positioned in their allotted stations. As for the people, I noticed that, some sort of expectation and excitement was visible on every face. I was received with warmth and respect everywhere though I could not miss the expression of curiosity on the faces of the villagers on seeing me there. I was a new comer from afar. However, I did not feel even for a moment that I was a stranger. In spite of the difference in language, way of life and climate, I could feel that we were one and shared a common ethos. I had moved thousands of kilometers from home, yet I was still at home. I tried to talk to a large number of people and also the polling officers. I could mostly manage with Hindi and English. The help of a translator was required on very few occasions. I was convinced that the people would be exercising their franchise in a free atmosphere. Almost at the end of the day's journey, I happened to meet the young District Collector, who stopped his vehicle on seeing my cavalcade. We chatted for sometime. It transpired that he had set out early in the morning and had visited every sensitive area of the District by that time. It was impressive. I got some useful tips from him before we parted company.

The hectic canvassing activities were already over the previous day. Calm had permeated the atmosphere. It was a calm, pregnant with the excitement of the day to follow. However, there was nothing in it to give even an inking of the spectacle that was to unfold the following day, which was the polling day. What I was to witness, was an expression of the free will of people, a timeless feeling which transcends the bounds of age and geography and is present, like atmosphere, wherever man lives whether he is white or black, rich or poor, literate or illiterate. I thus, lived a unique experience of life. I had never experienced this when I had cast my own vote. I returned to the Circuit House late in the evening. After having a refreshing shower and typical Assamese dinner, I went to sleep early with the strains of *Mian*

Ki Malhar of Ravi Shankar echoing in my mind. I had carried my Walkman and a few tapes along. By sheer co-incidence, it started raining around that time.

Next day, i.e. the 8th of June was the polling day. As arranged, the security staff and my driver came to the Circuit House at 6.00 a.m. I left immediately thereafter. I wanted to reach a polling station located in the interior and witness the very first vote being cast. I reached a station in Panery Assembly Constituency just in time. It was a school building. Long queues had already formed there and the ground in front was full of people. The very first vote cast was by a 75 years old lady who put her thumb impression on the counter foil of the ballot paper and was helped out in inserting the voting foil into the ballot box. After watching the process for sometime I moved to another polling station. The rest of the day was spent, barring the brief interruption of a hurried lunch and numerous cups of 'working tea', in visiting over 30 polling stations spread over the length and breadth of the three Assembly Constituencies. The scene everywhere was the same. The whole atmosphere was festive. Such buoyance in the people could have been witnessed only during Dussehra, X'Mas, Id or Bihoo. I could make this out from the sparkle in their eyes and the briskness of their pace. While we in the cities had been told that it was our sacred duty to cast our votes, for these village folk, casting of vote was a natural expression of an inner urge. No amount of persuasion, coercion or temptation could have drawn out so many people from every nook and corner of the area. Some of them had to walk a few miles to cast their votes. I could see them converging from every direction. These streams of people in this remote area were like the veins throbbing with life blood of democracy which kept these far-flung parts of the body-politic alive and alert. And what a display of colour! Whether it was a saree worn by an Assamese lady or the long skirt worn by a Bodo lady, it appeared that every hue that cotton or synthetic fibre could take on, had been used in their dress. The red, yellow and purple were particularly eye-catching. The people seemed truly electrified by this expression of their free will through ballot. They came alone or in groups, with family members or friends and all invariably clad in their best clothes. Each voter seemed to be conscious of the value of this small sheet of paper called ballot and how it got charged with immense energy, the moment the mark was put on it with a rubber stamp and was cast. Each of them was the face of freedom and democracy. This set off a reflective mood in me. I thought how even the most powerful empires in history have not been able to put shackles on this free will of man for long. So long as Pax Romana was the embodiment of the free will of its people, it spread far and wide and grew from strength to strength. However, when it became an instrument of oppression and destruction, the empire crumbled. This is the refrain of history. The spirit of freedom, even if extinguished, has, Phoenix like, revived again and again. We in India have a genuine democracy, a true reflection of the free will of its people. The fruits of economic and scientific progress may not have reached every one. Yet it is not uncommon to see that even a half-clad, half-fed man in the street or an illiterate man in the remote village can, by and large, question any action of the state and criticize the high and mighty without being hauled up or incarcerated. This is no mean achievement. However there is a small price to be paid for it: to maintain and to protect this freedom, each citizen has to willingly part with some of it for the good of all.

I returned to Udalguri town late in the evening. The ballot boxes from all the polling stations had been received in the Deputy Collector's office during the night. Next morning I met the Returning Officer. Excepting for one irregularity due to the inadvertence of one polling officer, which was promptly brought to the notice of the Election Commission by me, the things had gone well. People had cast their votes freely and fearlessly.

I left for Guwahati in the afternoon and reached there in the evening. I spent the night in the Old Circuit House located on the banks of Brahmaputra. As the day was fading, I heard the chorus of the birds from the nearby cluster of trees, announcing the passing of one more day. Sitting on a cane chair on the lawn of the Circuit House and gazing at the Brahmaputra in the twilight hours, my eyes captured the scene for perpetuity in my memory. I left for Delhi the next morning. I came back again to Udalguri for the counting of votes from 16th to 19th of June, 1991. It was a smooth affair, though quite tiring.

I was thankful to the Election Commission. But for it, I would have missed seeing a fascinating area and would have been deprived of a unique experience. I saw the making and functioning of the Democracy at the grass-roots as reflected in the unending queues at the polling booths, made up of masses—the poor not so poor and well off, illiterate, not so literate and educated, all alike, from near and far, thronging in large numbers to cast their votes without any inhibition or fear, thus contributing their bit to it, better than the denizens of the cities. And behind all this, was the invisible but palpable hand of Election Commission, with its new found identity.

CHAPTER 5

Port with a Past

I must confess that I had not heard the name Bheemunipatnam earlier. I had to feign knowledge of the place whenever the Customs Officers of Vizag Custom House talked about it with such familiarity that the knowledge on the part of the listener was taken for granted. However, during the course of my three days stay at Vizag, I had gleaned enough details of the place so as to talk about it with sufficient ease.

Bheemunipatnam is a sleepy port town now, but which must have been vibrant with maritime activity in not so distant a past. It was called Bimlipatnam during the British rule. As per the folklore prevalent in the area, it was named after Bheema, one of the Pandavas who, as per the legend, killed demon Bakasura on the hill which lies to the south of the town. It is quite likely that Bheemunipatnam was one of the ports on the east coast from which the ancient mariners had set out to the east and spread the Indian culture and religion to the far off lands of Thailand, Cambodia and Indonesia.

Little would they have realized that they were the ambassadors of Indian culture and religion and that their expeditions would leave such lasting impression in these areas that the world, even after 1000 years, would look with awe and admiration on the master pieces like Angkor Wat and Boro Bodur.

Bheemunipatnam is about 30 kms by road to the north east of Vishakhapatnam. As per the historical evidence, the Nizam of Hyderabad, with the approval of Mughal Emperor in Delhi gave Dutch "Kavulu" of the settlement at this place in the middle of 18th Century. However, the British East India Company took over the control of this Dutch settlement in 1781 or 1782. The old light house in the port, the dilapidated factories, the old cemeteries dating back to 17th and 18th centuries and a beautiful Roman Catholic Church, which is more than 100 years old, testify to the Dutch and English influence on the life and architecture of the place.

The activities of the port reached their zenith during the latter part of the19th century. The establishment of Ripley Company in 1854 by George Ripley helped in the development of the port as one of the busiest in the country at that time. Ripley Company used to export items like Bimli jute, Gopalpore hemp, Palmyra fibre, groundnut kernels etc. The port was reportedly handling more cargo than any other port on the east coast except perhaps Madras and Calcutta. A few other European companies and the three internationally renowned companies like Ralli Bros., Louis Dreyfus and East Asiatic company also used to export various items of merchandise through this port.

The onset of Second World War and in particular the departure of the British drew a curtain on the activities of the port, as the big companies left the place one by one. Ripley and Company were the last to leave in 1958. However, still operating from Vishakhapatnam, the company brought a ship called SS India Commerce to Bheemunipatnam on 15.11.1963 to load the cargo of jute. This was their last ship to load cargo from that port.

Vizag Custom House was the venue for one of the tariff conferences. Before leaving the conference hall., Shri B.V. Kumar the then Member (Customs), in the Central Board Of Excise And Customs, had mentioned that he would be visiting Bheemunipatnam Custom House, the next morning and asked some of us to come along.

Having heard about the place so much in the preceding two days I grabbed the offer.

We started in the morning when the air was still crisp. Bheemunipatnam is about half an hour's drive from Vizag. My curiosity increased as we were approaching the place. Our vehicle suddenly swerved to the left and emerged right near the sea shore. I could see the coconut groves along the beach as far as the eyes could reach. I could also see the distant high waves of the sea slowly becoming less menacing as they approached the shore and gently faded into the breakers lapping the wet sand. A few yards away from the place where we had stopped, was the Custom House Building, still withstanding the onslaught of time. It was a single storied building with a slanting roof covered with tiles.

The Custom House was spotlessly clean inside. It was kept airy and cool by the sea breeze coming through the large windows of the building. It had four rooms. The room on the right was of "Customs Collector". It was austerely furnished; but one could not miss the old heavy teakwood table which may have been used by the generations of Customs Collectors. I could visualize how the Customs Officer sitting behind this table, when fatigued with work, had only to turn his head a little to peep through the window and see the blue sea and gracefully moving catamarans and boats. Perhaps some other old Custom Houses in the country might be having a similar view. Perhaps the old and new Custom Houses in Bombay and Madras might have provided a similar view in the past. But all we can see today from these Custom Houses is the sight of crowded wharves and greenish and stagnant sea water; the real sea is invisible, somewhere in the background.

The second room of the building had an old wooden stand with a couple of muskets neatly fixed on it. The muskets also were the relics from the past. Another room of the Custom House had a safe which may have been used for keeping the day's collection of duty in the olden days. It had thick side walls and strong door and appeared to have been made somewhere in England.

The staff then presented some old records of the Custom House which had been carefully preserved for almost a hundred years. They instantly drew my attention. The entries in the old records of the Customs House related to the year 1905 or so. The writing was done, in some places by the famous but now extinct 'G' nib and at other places by a pen or a holder in blue-.black ink. Three of the entries in the register proved to be of great interest. These were authentic and unalloyed chips-albeit small, from the history. Two entries mentioned about the two notifications issued by the Governor General under the old Sea Customs Act, 1878, banning the entry of two books in praise of Mahatma Gandhi and Lala Lajpat Rai. The third entry related to a similar notification issued by the Governor of Madras Presidency banning the entry of a work concerning the exploits of the legendary freedom fighter from Andhra Pradesh—Shri A. Sita Ram Raju. Those were apparently adjudged as anti-national and subversive and the erstwhile Sea Customs Act was used as an instrument to keep a check on the activities of these leaders. It was clear that even in those days when the freedom struggle was at an incipient stage, these leaders commanded both awe and respect of the mighty empire.

There was simplicity, clarity and precision in the language of these registers. Some of the entries related to the standing instructions and circulars. One could perhaps know everything about the work of the Customs from these registers without reference to any other document. It appeared that many years' instructions had been kept capsuled in those registers. At that moment I was wondering how on numerous occasions I had to struggle to locate even recent clarifications and circulars of the department on classification and other matters, such is their frequency and volume. We have all the modern aids like computer, fax and other electronics gadgets to help us; yet we find that the process of the decision-making has not become less complex or easier. In our quest for perfection and the urge to keep pace with other nations and to meet the myriad demands of fast-changing trade and industry, we have given ourselves a system which is an ever enlarging skein. It is a system where basic provisions need clarification and the clarifications tend to become outdated too fast.

Is our system really superior to what the Customs Collector had at the turn of the century? I have been debating this since then. However, I am clear about one thing: clarity, precision and simplicity are qualities which are relevant at all times. We may use super computers in our office and other work, land in Mercury or go further into the cosmos, yet these qualities will be valid not only in the 21st Century but also in the 31st Century and beyond. These are in fact timeless. However, in our quest for rationalization and specialization, we seem to have lost touch with these basic things some where on the way.

CHAPTER 6

Journey to the Erstwhile Gateway of Nepal

THE remote city of Raxaul on the Indo-Nepal border always had a fascination as it is located in an area where Buddha was born and later wandered about as a mendicant till he got the ultimate wisdom under the Bodhi tree and gave his first sermon at Sarnath. Nearby places like Rajgir, Kapilvastu and Kushinagar are now part of Buddhist lore. The modern times have added some more significance to it as it is the main transit point between India and Nepal. In fact till 1950, this was the sole point to connect Nepal with the rest of the world through the city of Beergunj located in Nepal plains, across Raxaul.

Raxaul is the most important Customs Station on the Indian side for trade and transit to Nepal. Nearly half of the cargo coming from and going to Nepal passes through Raxaul.

During the middle of February in 1992, when the winter was receding and the spring was in the air, I went to Raxaul on an official errand. This was my first visit to Raxaul. I flew to Patna and after spending half a day in the Customs Office, I proceeded to Muzaffarpur by road on my way to Raxaul. There was nothing memorable about this portion of the journey, excepting the impressive sight of Ganga and Gandak from the bridge and the sight of Patna University buildings along the banks of Ganga. It was 8 p.m. when we reached Muzaffarpur. As the State Guest House was not available, I stayed in the Officers' Mess of NCC. The frugal look of the place was more than atoned by the warm reception extended by Col. Mohanty of NCC who also happened to be staying there. We had an interesting chat. Late through the evening when Col. Sharma of Army also joined us, I gathered that the mess is located in the middle of an open expanse of land called Gol Chakkar. It derives its name from its shape and the area is big enough to easily contain three parallel air strips. The land is grassy, dotted with a few trees and has some old houses in the middle and periphery, each having some interesting past. On the one side of it are the Circuit House, the commissioner's residence and some army barracks and on the other side an Officer's Mess and a Church which was constructed sometime in the early part of the century for the British Troops. The date of construction of the Mess, as inscribed on a stone, is 1914. And near the middle of the ground are two more bungalows. One of them, which used to be an armoury earlier, is now the residence of a serving Army Major. The other one is a recruiting office, which was earlier a briefing and debriefing office for the Air Force pilots during the war. About a third of the field was earlier used as an air field. The runway is still faintly visible on the land. Nobody was sure since when the area has been in the use of the Army. However, it continues to be associated with the Army. Barring the construction of a few houses on one edge of the field, urbanisation has not been able to nibble away much of its area.

Next morning I walked around at least half of the 'chakkar'. It was a refreshing walk. I noticed two hollow, tapering poles of steel about 10 ft. high in th middle of the vast ground. My enquiry with my host revealed that the two poles are the goal post of the Polo Ground which was located next to the air strip. The other two poles however have disappeared. The British army officers used to play polo on this ground.

Before leaving for Raxaul, I had a quick round of Muzaffarpur city. It was not different from any other cities of UP or Bihar, excepting for the impressive red brick building of Langat Singh College which is still the best known seat of learning in North Bihar. Acharya J.B. Kriplani was a lecturer there for sometime. The college building, though not in good shape, was still quite an impressive structure. I felt a bit sad but got quickly reconciled, thinking that in India, a structure is at its best at the inception and then deterioration sets in from the day one. Age bestows a unique beauty to the old structures. But it takes meticulous care to preserve that beauty.

It was good four hours' drive from Muzaffarpur to Raxaul. We touched Motihari town on the way. The road, which was quite broad but bumpy, took us through the lush green fields of wheat and mustard, irrigated by old Gandak river. We reached Raxaul around noon. The Land Customs Station here is located barely a few meters away from Nepal border. Large number of trucks full of cargo were lined up on the road, to cross over to Nepal after the Customs check. Most of the cargo was in transit from the port of Calcutta to Nepal. The Customs clearance was quick. Equal number of trucks were lined up on the other side of the Customs barrier. They contained cargo, either meant for India or in transit for export via Calcutta. I was a bit surprised to note that this road, which was so important as a trade route, passed through an old bridge just across the Customs barrier, broad enough to let only one truck pass at a time. A new bridge was however under construction. Small town of Raxaul seemed to be humming with activity. Similar activity was noticeable in the city of Beerganj in Nepal just across the border. For Nepal,

Beerganj Custom House collects about 50% of its Customs revenue. Raxaul and Beerganj are like twin cities with people moving to and from either side freely. And they are inter-dependent. People of Beerganj are dependent on Raxaul for most of their daily necessities and the people of Raxaul are dependent on Beerganj for things other than daily necessities!

Shankaracharya Dwar, Beergunj on Beergunj-Raxaul Road

After I reached Raxaul, I could not resist the urge of crossing the international border and derive the satisfaction of visiting one more country. I did it with such ease that I did not even realize it because the normal hassles associated with a foreign visit were totally absent here. I realized that I was in Nepal, only after I had walked up to Shankaracharya Gate which was about 200 metres inside Nepal on the road leading to Beerganj. The gate was quite an impressive structure built in typical Nepali tradition of architecture. I was informed that the gate was built to welcome the Shankaracharya from India when he visited Nepal. Such was the reverence for the sage in Nepal, at least till then. The year of construction as shown in the gate was Samvat 2044, which, I was told, corresponds to the year 1986. I took the photograph of the structure, spent some time on the spot and then returned to India!

I spent the rest of the day in the Land Customs Station, examining the various matters relating to Customs revenue and procedure.

With the day's work behind me, I went to the Guest House where I was to spend the night. This place is known as the Embassy Guest House. It is located in a walled compound covering an area of more than20 acres. The outer gate of the compound is located just behind the Land Custom Station The drive-way leads to yet another stone gate deep inside, close to the Guest House building. One cannot miss the dark green creeper covering most part of the gate like ivy. Three fourth of the guest house compound is covered by mango groves, where the spread of many trees exceeded their height and thus gave the appearance of big green canopies. The lower branches of many such trees almost touched the ground. The area in front of the Guest House had a well maintained garden and a variety of large trees, both in front and on both sides of the Guest House. I found, the Guest House building and its surroundings very captivating. The Guest House is a single-storied rectangular building with a flat roof, simple and belies the beauty of its interior. The building, which stood on a five feet high platform, was approachable from the ground by a flight of about four steps. It had a broad veranda on three sides which is fenced by a sturdy wooden grill of simple design, about 2.5 ft. in height. Apart from the common dining hall, it had two suites of three rooms each on either wing. The first two rooms of the suite were of about 20 ft. × 20 ft. size and had equally high ceiling.

The third room was however, smaller. The first room was a living room with a stone fire place and a wooden mantel-piece over it. All rooms had ventilators near the ceiling in perfect working condition and there was a strip of wood in the middle of all the four walls of the rooms, perhaps for aesthetic effect. The doors with teak frame and glass panel were about 8 ft. high and the windows were smaller but of same design. The brass latches in the doors were particularly eye-catching with their 18" length. The doors had old fashioned round brass knobs also. There was one wooden almirah each in the rooms for clothes etc. which was embedded in the wall, topped by slanting, roof-like shade of wood. In addition, there was a eight-sided small side-table, a rack and a clothes' stand, all made of thick wood in simple classic mould where the teak had been sawn and hewed into shapes of raw beauty. These were from a different age. The doors and windows were well protected by dark brown polish. The whole place was well kept and neat. The place did not have any signs of decadence. This was a museum piece, as houses like this are not built any more. Modern economics is against them.

I took a round of the compound when it was dusk. The murmur of leaves, swayed by the evening breeze mingled with the chorus of birds from the massive Pipal tree nearby. I could also notice the trees of Neem, Mango, Shisham, Gulmohar and a solitary Semel tree which was tallest of them all, full of red flowers in its leafless branches, its typical feature at that time of the year. Through a small gap in the compound wall in front of the guest house, I could see beyond the wheat and mustard fields stretching right upto Nepal border. The atmosphere had a quietness and magic about it. The place was no longer new for me and I felt that I had always known it for a long time. It was familiar yet different. It was a microcosm of Indian milieu, which through the ages has been woven into our art, literature and music, in shapes, colours and rhythms of infinite variety.

After dinner I called the caretaker, Shri Kapil Dev Babu for a chat. He was living in a house in the compound—a part of the Indian Embassy in Kathmandu. However, he had been staying there for the last nine years. The Guest House itself is the property of the Indian Embassy in Kathmandu. It was constructed by the British about 100 years back for the use of the British Ambassador at Kathmandu as a transit camp. I was informed that the Ambassador used to come down to the Guest House for about 3 months every winter. During this period, his dak used to be brought to him by the runners from Kathmandu. The Ranas of Nepal also used to camp in the Guest House whenever they came for hunting in the nearby Tarai Jungles. The 'astabal' (sheds for keeping the horses) was still in-tact in the compound. Its use had however changed. The first British Ambassador to occupy the Guest House was Col. Betham and the first Indian Ambassador was Shri S.S. Majithia. Surprisingly, the old Guest House Register of the period had been preserved. With the direct flights available to Kathmandu, the present day Indian ambassadors take aerial route these days.

I plumed myself over the thought of sleeping in the same room in which the plenipotentiaries of the British empire had stayed in the years by-gone.

It was quite intriguing to know from Kapil Dev Babu that prior to 1957, there was no through road from Raxaul upto Kathmandu. Air connections were still a long way off. Raxaul was connected with Amlihganj, about 45 km away by a narrow-gauge train. Amlihganj was further connected with Bhempeti by a narrow road where only small buses could ply. From Bhempeti toThankot one had to walk about 30 kms. The distance of about 15 kms from Thankot to Kathmandu was again connected by road where small buses used to ply. There was a rope-way from Bhimpeti to Thankot for carrying cargo. Today there is a direct and broad road linking Raxaul with Kathmandu.

As I wanted to visit Bithamore and other Customs

formations east of Raxaul, I chose a different route for my return journey to Patna. The shortest route to these places was via Beerganj and Janakpur, both in Nepal. We left next morning after obtaining necessary permits for our vehicles at Beerganj. It took about 4 hours to reach Janakpur and another one hour to Bithamore. The road is broad and good and is called Rajpath and goes further to the eastern extremity of Nepal. It mostly runs parallel to foot-hills of Nepal passing through numerous bridges constructed by Russian Engineers in the seventies. The villages on the way were few and far between and the traffic extremely thin. The forest all along was thick and apparently undespoiled. More people and vehicles were noticeable as we approached Janakpur. It is believed that Raja Janak's capital was located here. The present temple at Janakpur is however of recent origin. The temple complex contained wall paintings and statues depicting the various episodes of Ramayana. The place was full of visitors from India and Nepal.

A little beyond Janakpur, I entered the Indian border and reached Bithamore and I was back to my routine, with, of course, memories of the brief visit which I would later recall, to enliven dull moments.

CHAPTER 7

Malwa Diary—I (Gwalior)

IT was the first day of September 1992, the month which gives the first feeble but clearly perceptible signals denoting the end of a long and hot summer and humid rainy season and heralds the beginning of the short Indian autumn followed by a longer winter. A few, near-transparent fluffs of clouds, scattered, and clearly visible against the blue and bright sky, were rushing, as though shy of the sun-light and in a hurry to disappear behind the horizon. I had intended to set out on my official trip around this time after the rains was over, though its magic lingers on in the vegetation all over the plains and hills of north India.

I had travelled by Shatabdi Express on two earlier occasions; to Lucknow and to Bhopal. Both the times, the journey was very enjoyable. This time, though my destination was Indore, the heart of Malwa, I had planned a stop over at Gwalior and Bhopal. I preferred travel by Shatabdi to flying, as the experience reminded me of my journeys by Shin-Kan-Sen (Bullet train) in Japan. However, the clock-work precision and frequency with which the Shin-Kan-Sen runs (one in less than every 10 minutes) is still a far cry for us. The Shatabdi is a promising start which deserves kudos, though it has a long way to go, to be anywhere near the international standards.

I was looking forward to several hours of quiet journey. One of the most enjoyable pastime for me is reading books during train journeys. In fact the last time I had done some good reading during a train journey was 25 years back when, I had travelled by Frontier Mail on a couple of occasions between Bombay and Delhi during the training. Even upto late sixties the Frontier was at least as good as a perfect carbon copy of its former grandeur. According to old timers, Frontier's run during its heydays was so smooth, that a glass of water kept on table in the first class cabin, would not spill and a coin kept on it would not move even by a hair's breadth through the journey. And it had to be so, as it was not only the pride of Indian Railways in the olden times but also the Raj's lifeline upto the north western frontier, right upto Afghan border, helping it to ferry its elite troops.

The train left New Delhi station at 6.15 a.m. sharp. Gwalior was my first stop as I had some official work there and reached Gwalior at 9.30 a.m. I was a bit excited even as the train was some miles away from Gwalior when the Fort of Gwalior, slowly emerged from the horizon, first as a massive boulder with blurred outlines and then a little later, in its full glory, with Man Mandir and Sas-Bahu Temple, clearly silhouetted against the clear and blue autumn sky. I got the feel of the Malwa ambience with this view of the massive Fort from a distance, though the real Malwa lay well beyond Gwalior. I was posted in Gwalior in 1969-70 as circle officer of Central Excise, a post long since extinct. This time, while having a keen look at the Fort from the train, I discovered that a new white structure had been added to the Fort, a

Gurudwara which I later came to know was built after 1970. It was a pleasant surprise to find that Gwalior Station was as clean as it used to be during the earlier days, and time seemed to have stood still for its beautiful stone structure.

A feeling of regret had always remained with me for not having my fill of what the city of Gwalior has to offer. And it has plenty to offer. In fact, Gwalior is one of the few Indian cities like Delhi, Kolkata or Varanasi of which one can never have too much. I had visited Gwalior Fort possibly twice during my posting which was for a little over one year but did not capture its beauty for my reminiscence as I had no camera at that time. Being a restricted item of import, attracting very high import duty, it was still a prized possession of a select few. My other regret was that I could attend only one of the two Tansen Samaroh celebrated during my stint. I wanted to make up this time, as much as I could, at least by visiting some of its famous sites.

Having finished the official work in the forenoon, I set out in the afternoon and spent my time till late in the evening amidst the famous monuments of the city. I first went to the

Mausoleum of Mohammad Shah Ghause at Gwalior

Mausoleum of Mohd. Shah Ghause and Samadhi of Tansen and took the photographs in perfect sun-light. The former is a medieval structure in sandstone, blackened by moss at several places. It is from the platform of this impressive structure that classical musicians from all over the country perform for three to four days every year to pay their homage to Tansen. I briefly sat by the tamarind tree in front of Tansen's Samadhi, which is a small but beautiful sandstone

Samadhi of Tansen at Gwalior

structure by the side of the mausoleum. Local people believe that the tree dates back to Tansen's time. From there I made straight for the Fort around 4 p.m. There had been a heavy down pour sometime earlier and some drizzling was still continuing. As we crossed Rani Jhansi Statue, the vehicle had to wade through knee-deep water, which had flooded into the road from the nullah emnating from the Gwalior Fort. This is the same nullah near which, as per the local lore, the Rani had perished while fighting the British. As we neared the Fort, I could notice numerous water-falls, formed instantly by the downpour, with white foamy water gushing out from the passages in the turret of the Fort. These falls are short-lived, making their brief appearance with each heavy shower and disappearing shortly thereafter. The vegetation on the outer slopes of the Fort, thick and lush green round the year, is at its best during and just after the monsoons.

My first stop there was Gujari Mahal, located at the bottom of the Fort. The Mrignayani serial in the T.V. around that time, had given the monument an added air of romance. This is a palace, which Raja Man Singh, who was a popular King in the medieval times had constructed for his favourite queen—a Gujari lady. Though a single storied structure, it looked like a double storied building because of the high foundation wall on the front side of the building. It gave an appearance of a small fortress. And to make the semblance complete, there is a big stone gate, flanked by mini-ramparts which has to be crossed for reaching the palace. After passing through the gate and walking few steps, one reaches the palace by a flight of stairs. Inside this structure there are several rooms which form a courtyard with open space in the middle. The building presently is used as a museum, which is quite well kept, with a number of rare and antique stone statues. After seeing this Palace we drove round the Fort and reached the top from the eastern entrance. To me this fort is one of the best-kept in India. The area enclosed by the massive walls of the Fort had been transformed by the monsoon into a vast green stretch of land dotted with numerous trees, big and small. The Fort commands panoramic view of the city, particularly from the Sas-Bahu Temple. The cluster of palaces down in the city at some distance, including one in use by the Scindia family, is clearly visible to the naked eye from the Fort. I did however, take snaps of near-by Man Mandir—the palace of Raja Man Singh, and Sas-Bahu temple, a structure of considerable craftsmanship and elegance. The chowkidar on duty there told us that the real name of the temple was Sahastra Bahu;

but with the passage of time the name had changed to 'Sas Bahu'. Both these monuments, the fort and the temple appeared to be well looked after, as there was no accumulation of rubble around, and dust inside. Also missing was the foul smell of bats, so common in many derelict monuments of the country. I spent another hour here, walking around monuments and the playgrounds of the Scindia School located in one portion of the vast flatland of the Fort, and then left with the hope that I may come again when the the sky is brighter.

CHAPTER 8

Malwa Diary—II (Bhopal and Sanchi)

I left Gwalior by Shatabdi in the morning next day. The journey time of over 4 hours upto Bhopal was divided between reading Mark Tully's 'There is No Full Stop in India' and looking through the window at the undulating landscape of Malwa plateau revitalised by the monsoon, as it unfolded like a film from the moving train. Both were highly enjoyable. The high point of the journey was a view of the Stupa of Sanchi, atop that wooded hillock. I have had the glimpse of this structure several times in the past through the window of the passing train. However on each occasion I had looked at it with a feeling of curiosity and wonder. I had always wished to climb the hill and walk upto the stupa and touch this ancient structure. This long cherished wish was fulfilled this year—a unique year for me because during this visit to Bhopal I was able to see not only Sanchi, but also the nearby caves of Gupta period, Bhim Baithaka and the unfinished Siva temple of Raja Bhoj's time.

I was able to leave for Sanchi around 4 p.m. with enough time to breathe and feel the ambience of the place a little longer, my official engagements at Bhopal being brief. This time I had come equipped with my Nikon also. For me this wooded hillock, with its unique stone structure, is one of the most beautiful sites in India. It is a rare blend of history and nature, the stupa epitomising a glorious period of India's past and the hillock, no more than a mile in circumference, with plenty of thick-leaved Phiranee trees and other vegetation typical of Malwa plateau, is a place of rare beauty. It started raining heavily when we reached Sanchi but as we reached the top of the hillock, the downpour subsided into a gentle drizzle. But further down in the fields at some distance, I could see the heavy showers still continuing, visible against the backdrop of a grey sky, and waving like a giant gossamer curtain in the wind, right upto the horizon. We took shelter in the ancient stone temple near the main stupa as it had no shelter, being a solid stone structure without any hollow space. The rain stopped as suddenly as it came. The sky however remained overcast. The light was still inadequate. I took some photographs anyway. The only other people in the area were a group of Srilankans who were busy taking group photographs. They seemed to be overwhelmed by their visit to this place. After the group departed, only Satish, my colleague from Bhopal and I were left in the area. Quietness of the place then started growing on us. We remained there for about an hour, walking around the main stupa, the smaller stupa and newly built Buddhist temple nearby respectively. The plateau and the fields around us, as far as the eye could see, were clothed in resplendent green.

The time spent near the stupa was like a living dream. I kept on musing at the simple but solemn beauty of the stone structure. Though a man-made structure, it had become one with the milieu, the rocks, the trees and the surrounding air—a timeless phenomenon. It is associated with two of the greatest personages of Indian and world history—of whom one was monk, the Enlightened one, whose preachings spread, crossing the Himalayas, the oceans and vast land masses, across several empires and kingdoms thousands of miles away, not at the point of sword, but with a message of love and peace. And they have endured. And the other, his disciple, was an emperor of the biggest empire in Indian history, spreading from Gandhar and Taxsila in the north to Madurai in the south. It has withstood, the ravages of time. The monument, supposed to be having the relics of Buddha, looks refreshingly shipshape even after two thousand five hundred years. Humanity measures time by its own standards. The human civilisation, as we know it, is about 4 to 5 millenniums old. And in the context of the cosmos even a million years is no more than a split second. However by the standards of this tiny planet, a millennium or two border on immortality. Seen against cosmos and eternity which are endless and timeless, nothing on earth can be called

The Asoka Stupa at Sanchi

permanent or immortal, even if it lasts a few million or even billion years. But one cannot but extol the brave attempts of the gifted and brave men through the ages who had tried to defy time, even though briefly, by carving out a Sphinx or putting up a Parthenon or the only man-made structure visible from the moon or by honing the chunks of raw marble into shapes of delicate beauty, which have lasted a few millenniums and are still there, mesmerizing the humanity by their beauty. Sanchi Stupa is one such attempt to defy time, an attempt to reach out to eternity and cosmos, a byte in the infinite memory of timelessness, which cannot be deleted.

CHAPTER 9

Malwa Diary—III (Mandu and Ujjain)

THE spell cast by Sanchi continued to linger on, long after I had reached the Guest House of the Communication Deptt., atop the ridge in new Bhopal. It is a cosy place providing a panoramic view of new Bhopal.

The next day we left Bhopal at about 6 a.m. by road. It was a typical Malwa morning, crisp and clear. We passed by the Raj Bhawan and the old city, getting a good view of the minarets, the mosques, and the western extremity of Bhopal lake. Even after we had reached the open country side, the lake remained within the view for a long time as we moved towards Indore.

We reached Indore at about 12 a.m., some delay having been caused by mechanical problem in the vehicle, which was attended to at Dewas, the city of Kumar Gandharva. I went straight to the office of the Collector of Central Excise (as the Commissioner was then called), at Manick Bagh palace to attend to my work. This palace had been purchased by the Department. from the Indore royal family some years back. It is a stately structure of stone, with very high ceilings and surrounded by a garden, a few acres in area, which unfortunately has now a seedy look, but not without the signs of its old grandeur. While in the Collector's room, I was charmed by a large map of India, wrought in metal and plastered to the wall, demarcating the borders of the erstwhile State of Holkars.

I had always yerned to spend a night at Mandu, near one of its numerous lakes. My last visit to the place was a hurried daytime visit, lasting a few hours only.

I joined Shri Tampi, the Collector, who was also scheduled to proceed to a place close to Mandu on official work. We left around 4.30 p.m. It was history all the way, as we talked or gazed, during the intervals, at the green expanse of Malwa. This is one of the most beautiful countryside I have seen and its pleasant and mild climate and gentle evening breeze even at the height of summer, makes it a unique region. It is difficult to choose between the beauty of its evenings and mornings. The lay of the land is however eloquent about the evenings of Malwa.

Shri Tampi stopped at two places for his official work on the way and we reached Mandu around sun set for our overnight stay. M.P. Government's tourist cottage had been booked for us. There are several of these cottages by the side of the lake. Each cottage has two independent living suites. The place was clean and furnished with essentials. The surroundings had plenty of trees. In fact my cottage was half covered by the canopy of huge Phirnee tree and was the closest to the lake, being almost on its edge. At the opposite end of the lake, beyond which the mountains formed the back drop, I could see a cluster of lotus flowers, and further on, the lake merged with the green paddy fields. It was difficult to discern from this end, where the lake ended and the paddy-fields commenced. The lake had turned golden in the dying light of the day. We sat for long below the canopy of the phirnee tree near my cottage. The evening then turned pleasantly cold.

When it was dark, we drove upto Roopmati's pavilion, on top of the hill on the western side. People here still talk about the romance of Baj Bahadur, Sultan of Malwa in medieval times, and Roopmati. The road gently winds upto the top of the hill. However, on reaching the pavilion about 3 kms up in the hill, we noticed that the other face of this hillock dropped rather vertically into the plains where, in Roopmati's time Narmada must have had its course. This was the spot, as per the lore, to which Roopmati used to come every day in the morning to have a glimpse of the Narmada. She was its ardent devotee. Baj Bahadur had built this pavilion at that spot for Roopmati. This also appeared to be the highest point of Mandu. Baj Bahadur's Palace is located in the valley just below this hill. When we reached the pavilion, the visibility was very poor as the sky was overcast and there was mist around. The distant lights of Dharampuri, appeared to be

Rani Roopmati's pavilion, Mandu, in the monsoon mist

glowing rather feebly from here. Narmada was however not visible and the guide told us that it could be seen like a thin white line only on a clear and moonlit night.

We returned to the cottage after half an hour and had our dinner in the nearby restaurant which was part of the tourist complex and then retired to our respective cottages. By this time Mandu had turned in to a hill station. It was chilly.

The next day we set out at 6 a.m. to have a look at various monuments of Mandu. Mandu hills, after being washed and nourished by the just receded monsoons, looked green and fresh at that hour. The Roopmati Pavillion at a distance was getting frequently enveloped by the rolling mass of thick fog. We first drove to Rani Roopmati's pavilion. While in the pavilion, we saw bits of fog passing through it several times and occasionally covering it completely. I however succeeded in taking some snaps of the pavilion during the intervals. The pavilion commands a panoramic view of Mandu hills and the Narmada plains below. From the pavilion, we drove to Baj Bahadur's Palace in the valley at the bottom of the same hill. Our knowledgeable guide poured out all that he knew about Baj Bahadur and Rani Roopmati. He also took us to the first floor of the Palace where, at one end there is a rather long and narrow room with low platform, on either end, facing each other. As per the lore, Roopmati used to sing from one of the platforms and Baj Bahadur used to listen from the other at the opposite end. Roopmati was an accomplished musician and singer and Baj Bahadur a cognoscente of art and music. In fact it was music which had brought Baj Bahadur and Roopmati close. Our guide further informed that the said room was specially constructed for perfect acoustic effect. He tried to prove the point by singing a few lines from one platform while we listened from the other. Even though he deliberately sang in near whisper, yet every word of what he sang came out in staccato notes. He proved his point.

From the Palace, we moved to the marble tomb of Hoshangshah, Jahaz Mahal and the Shiva temple.

Jahaz Mahal is located in idyllic surroundings. Though some portions of it have given way, yet what remains is reasonably well kept. It has two lotus shaped swimming pools at two floors, one on the first and the other on the second. The pools have two levels—one about 8 feet deep and the other 4 feet—both joined by stone steps and are about 15 × 15 ft in size. These, we were told, were fed from the nearby well from where the water was drawn to a considerable height by a 'rahat' and then channelised first to the swimming pool on the higher level and from there to the lower swimming pool. The real beauty of the Palace however lay in its two ponds, one in front—a man-made pond, surrounded by well laid out gardens and the other at the back of the palace, which was much bigger and natural. It is this lake which gives the unique name to the palace. In the monsoon season, when the natural lake at the back of the palace is full to the brim, the palace gives a look of a ship afloat on the water. The

Tomb of Hoshang Shah at Mandu

man-made structures here are in absolute harmony with nature, blending into a perfect whole.

I had missed the marble mausoleum of Hoshang Shah during my last visit to Mandu. The marble of the impressive building has been blackened by moss at several places. It has however survived well as a whole, in all its medieval splendour. Our guide told us that the architect of Taj Mahal, which followed a 100 years later, had come here to pay homage to his great predecessor and had drawn inspiration from this monument.

The Shiva temple has been carved out of horizontal face of the rock cliff. The Shiva linga is perennially bathed by a stream emanating from a crevice in the rock, just above the temple. From this spot one gets a picturesque view of the Mandu hills. The spot is reported to have caught the fancy of Akbar the Great, to whom the construction of the temple in its present shape is attributed. Our guide pointed out the inscription on the upper face of the temple in Persian, which records the visit of Akbar to this place and which, freely translated, would read: "If any one could get rest and peace even for a few moments at the place, he would consider his endeavour in constructing the place as successful."

We returned to our cottage around 11 a.m. and after taking a light breakfast, left Mandu around 11.30 a.m. We reached Indore at 1 p.m. I took leave of Govind Thampi in his office and left for Ujjain and reached around 3 p.m. and spent the evening in the ghats and temples.

This was my second visit to Ujjain. I had been to Ujjain sometime in 1970. The memories of the first visit had provided the impetus for this visit. The pleasure of going to a known place like Ujjain is something unique. As we pass by the known objects, buildings, lanes, the memories and past associations, dormant for long, are drawn from the recesses of the mind and flashed in the mind's screen.

I had always remembered Ujjain as a quiet city, it's temples thronged by devotees all day, it's markets lively and bustling with activity—a city conscious of its great past. It somehow escaped my notice on the previous occasion that the city has fairly broad and good roads and very little traffic congestion. I however distinctly remembered that the green countryside commenced right from the outskirts of the city. The familiar sites of any other Indian city—pools of dirty water, cluster of jhuggies and mounds of rubbish on the road-side, were conspicuous by their absence here. Ujjain had not changed with the passage of time.

There was little change in its ghats too. Perhaps they were cleaner than before. We went to Ranighat first. Shri Dubey, my colleague from the Department, who had volunteered to give me company, mentioned that the place had been spruced up and the bed of the river Kshipra, near the ghat had been cleaned and deepened just before the Kumbh in June, 1992. He also told me that the members of Daudi Vohra community of Ujjain had given Shramdan (voluntary and free service) for several days to deepen the Ranighat part of the river bed. Shramdan involved undertaking the strenuous and rather risky task of diving under the water by several young men of that community for many days. This event seemed to have been entirely missed by the media. I came to know about it because of my chance visit to this ghat. And it is doubtful if anyone outside Ujjain knows about it. Distrust, bitterness, violence and feeling of revenge between various communities seem to have so ossified the sensitivities of the people and thickened their skin, not only in this country but in many places elsewhere in the world, that communal rage and killing of innocents are becoming routine affairs, just one of the variants of normal human behaviour, surprising few and shocking even fewer. What happened in Kshipra, seems to belong to another planet, and such extra-planetary acts, though so few, do remind us that selfless and self-denying acts, civilities and tolerance have not after all entirely disappeared from the face of the earth. They are not alien to Indian ethos either.

Ujjain is one of the most important among the historical and holy cities of India. Yet it has very few old structures to boast of. However, it is rich in legend, concerning the lives of Vikramaditya and Kalidasa. All these legends have contrived to weave a magic around several temples. Some of them, according to the local lore, were the 'Ishth' Devtas of Kalidasa and Vikramadatya. The Bhairav temple, located at a lonely spot on the opposite bank of Kshipra, under a cluster of trees, where I witnessed liquor being poured on the stone deity by the devotees of the Lord, and which I was told is done, as per age-old custom, during different times of the day, conjured up an eerie and mysterious atmosphere of famous Betaal stories even at that time of the day.

Next day I attended to my office work and thereafter tried to make the best of whatever remained of the day. Shri Dubey, again accompanied me for the outing. He seemed to be well conversant with the folklores and the outlay of the city.

The temple of Mahakal was my first destination. I had

Mahakal Temple, Ujjain

some vague recollection of the place. The whole area, the approach to the temple and the compound of the temple was very clean. I reached the level of the temple after descending a sufficiently long flight of stone steps. River Kshipra, though very near to the temple, was not visible from the temple premises. Unlike other temples in the country, where the significance of the place itself completely overshadows the size and shape of the structure, Mahakal temple, though very important for Hindus, is also a beautiful piece of architecture. Its stone, blackened by passage of time, is similar to that of Raj Rajeshwara temple at Tanjore.

The other ghats of Kshipra were next in my itinerary. This small river, with dark, almost stagnating water, with its banks forming two almost parallel lines, as it passes through the city, with meadows or agricultural fields commencing right from the water line, had impressed me immensely by its endearing beauty.

Late in the evening I went back to the Guest House. The serenity of the city and the Kshipra seemed to have grown on me by that time.

This city has a soul. Many old cities of the world have it too. It is the new cities of today, where it is missing, because the soul of a city—like pearl in a shell, takes long to evolve, sometimes even three thousand years, as is the case with Varanasi, or even Ujjain.

CHAPTER 10

Where It Dawns in the Wee Hours

UNLESS the compulsions of profession or personal circumstances so dictate, most of us tend to move within a small area, close to one's abode or place of vocation. We however keep on hearing and reading about the diversity of India. There is a world of difference between knowing about this diversity through word of mouth or print and feeling and experiencing it by actually visiting the diverse places. Knowing is superficial and ephemeral. Feeling and experiencing leave a permanent imprint in the psyche. In spite of being aware about this unique diversity, we always tend to rush back to our shells—no sooner than we have set out of it. The shell becomes our world. To have the feel of our diversity is altogether a different proposition. It calls for some effort, some openness of mind and a will to come out of our shell, as it were, for long enough. The experience which then follows, has a permanence about it. No amount of reading and audio visual presentation can achieve what even brief meeting with people or a fleeting visit to a place can do. That is why, every visit to a new place and every meeting with people there, almost always results in some change in the set views or pre-conceived notions about it. The knowledge earlier gained through word of mouth or print, is, more often than not, proved wrong by subsequent experience. My visits to the diverse areas of the country have given me experience—by no means ample, yet good enough to correct many of my wrong notions. They have also given me a feeling of belonging to the whole country.

People fond of travelling in India, mostly choose North, South or West. Very few go to the East. And East for most of them ends with Calcutta or Bhubneshwar or in exceptional cases Guwahati & Shillong. Northeast still remains a distant and unfamiliar land, an amorphous blur in the consciousness of most of the people. The political situation and by modern standards, inadequate transport facilities in the area, have contributed to this to a great extent. However, the biggest hindrance has been the shell—syndrome. I have myself been guilty of it as my first visit to that area was in discharge of an official obligation—my duty as a Central Observer for the election from the Majabat Constituency in Assam in 1991. Having crossed the Brahmaputra and having breathed the crisp air of the foothills of Bhutan—an air filled with the gurgle of numerous mountain streams, during that visit, I had a strong urge to see this prism of the Northeast comprising several states in the Eastern extremity of India, a little more closely and extensively. It was official work again which took me to two of the states of North East—Manipur and Sikkim. And in the bargain, I also managed to go to Kalimpong and Darjeeling. After several postponements, I finally fixed 16.11.92 as the date of commencement of my journey to Imphal, the capital of Manipur. The flight departed pretty early, at 5.40 a.m. We had a brief halt at Calcutta and Guwahati. From Guwahati to Imphal the plane overflew the entire mountain ranges of that area, viz. Garo, Khasi, Jayantia and Lusai hills. This was my first view of these mountain ranges from such close proximity. It was a kaleidoscope of endless ranges, covered with dense forests and marked by thin, meandering lines of the rivers flowing through the narrow valleys between the mountains, like a necklace of light green jades spaced from each other, in a silver string, lying rather irregularly on the ground. And after some time, I suddenly noticed, through a gap in the mountains, a sprawling Valley merging with the distant hills in the eastern horizon. As the aeroplane swerved towards the gap and started descending, the outlines of the big city in the Valley became clear. I was told by a co-passenger that this was Imphal, the capital of Manipur. The Valley, I was told later, was about 100 kms long and 20-25 kms wide. This is the Valley where a unique culture, Indian in essence, yet subtly different in appearance, has developed through the centuries. The plane landed at 11.15 am. I was met at the airport by Shri Goswami, Asstt. Collector of Customs & Excise, Imphal and Nungshi Singh from Directorate of Revenue Intelligence. On my way to office, I gathered information about the place, people and the climate, in addition to official matters such as concentration of factories, problem of smuggling across the Indo-Burma Border etc. There are hardly any manufacturing units or factories in Manipur. A few small units are there in Dimapur, Nagaland. The agriculture and forests dominate the economy of the area which, on the positive side, mean a clean and unpolluted environment. I had mixed feelings over this. The problems of insurgency, drug-trafficking and addiction are too well known to be missed by anyone. Because of the insurgency, the tension in the area was too palpable—with the para-military forces visible or on the move everywhere. The roads in the city of Imphal, criss-crossing each other mostly at right angles, had considerable traffic of all kinds—cars, cycles, tempos, trucks and motorcycles along with the vehicles of the police and para-military forces. In contrast to the cities elsewhere in India, excepting Gujarat, lots of ladies were seen driving mopeds. However, the bustling activities of the day were in stark contrast to the gnawing silence of the evening. I found the roads and streets almost deserted immediately after sun set. This was a forced constriction of daily routine for a lively and energetic people, the people, with a long martial tradition. Their wiry, agile and fit figures are a testimony of this legacy. Yet these people, who had been wielding the sword and the spear with lethal efficacy, also know, not only how to hold a pen or a brush or a stringed instrument but also to hold them delicately so as to create masterpieces of shapes sounds and colours. The Valley has been a cradle of unique culture. One however feels a bit confused and concerned about the present. But it may be only a question of time before the east starts glittering again.

My official engagements were over by 4 p.m. After having a wash at the Circuit House—the only place of stay for visiting officials, I set out with my companion and guide, Shri Nungshi Singh to make the best of the remaining two odd hours before the onset of night, as it starts getting dark around 5 pm itself.

We went to the war memorial first, which is located in the heart of the city. It has thousands of graves of British officers and soldiers who died fighting the Japanese army in the Northeast during World War-II. It is not known what the Japanese did with their soldiers who perished there. All the graves appear to be identical and built in a symmetrical order. The difference lay in the prayers and messages from the kith and kin of the dead, engraved on each one of them in metal plaques. In addition, each grave contains, apart from the name of the deceased, the date of birth and the regiment to which he belonged. Most of them had died young, between the age of 19 and 35. One inscription on the grave of a Captain, aged 23 years read: "We miss you at the Grange". This was long back—in 1945. These people from the Grange, carrying the burden of this sad memory must themselves be old or dead by now. These few words including 'Grange' had that melancholic ring from the masterpiece of Emily Bronte.

From the cemetery we proceeded to see the Govind and Hanuman temples. On the way we passed through the palace of the King—a two storied structure only partly visible from the road. It was closed to the public. One can however have a glimpse of it from the road. It has a flattish dome, with rectangular base and a balcony below it. This was typical architecture of the east and reminded me of the dome of Kamakshi temple. As for the temples, both were small structures compared to the temples elsewhere in India. The main structures were totally overshadowed by the big assembly halls in front of them. They were distinct as they did not have the tapering high domes of the temples in the rest of India.

From the temples, we moved to have a quick run of the city. All the while Nungshi and I talked about the past and present of Manipur, the slow pace of development in the area

View of the palace at Imphal

and the problem of insurgency, drugs etc. I was impressed by his awareness of the problems. During the talks I gathered that total population of the State was about 18 lacs, the majority being Maitis, as the Hindus of the place call themselves, and Krishna their most popular deity. Nagas and Kukis are the other two main minorities of the state. They are Christians. Maities live in the plains and Nagas and Kukis come from the surrounding hills. It was a surprise to learn that one of the best polo teams in the country comes from Manipur. Manipur also hosts an annual polo tournament. Polo has been played by the martial Kshatriyas of Manipur for ages.

17th November 1992 turned out to be a memorable day and I had the feel of what I believe to be the essence of Manipur's life.

My official engagement with the State Govt. officials could be fixed only for the afternoon next day. We therefore decided to leave for the Logtak lake early in the morning. We left at 6 am. The town and the countryside were long awake by that time. I was told that dawn breaks in these parts around 4 a.m. as the place is located in the eastern extremity of India and we have a common time zone for the whole country. Within 15 minutes we crossed the outskirts of the city and moved into the open countryside. After about half an hour's drive we were in the proximity of the great lake and once near it, the lake seemed to cover and dominate the entire Valley. It was pleasantly cold as it was just the beginning of winter. I was told that Manipur is colder than Delhi during the winter. We passed through small markets and several villages on the way. The houses were mostly single storied and cottage type with a variety of crotons and flower plants in the open space around. The ladies wear typical Manipuri cotton sarees or gown. Naga shawl is used both by ladies and men and is the main protection against the cold. Men mostly wore kurta and dhoti in the brahmin style. On the way, we stopped for a while at Vishnu Puri village to see the old temple. It was a small red brick temple, with a small gate and an ASI notice indicating that it was a protected monument, being of historical importance. Its main structure was few meters high with four faces, a miniature of any north Indian temple. From this place we followed the old Indo-Burma road to see the INA memorial. The memorial is located a short distance away from the main road. The road leads to Churachandpur and further to Indo-Burma border. This was the main road and perhaps the only motorable road to Burma before 1947. From this point, the lake which looked like a single and vast sheet of water so far, now turned into numerous patches of water loosely joined together. This was because of numerous floating islands in the lake, many of which have crops in them and look like giant pieces of agricultural land broken away from the main-land and drifted into the waters of the lake. Some floating islands have tall grass and other wild vegetation too.

As pre-arranged, we reached the forest guest house located at some height in a hillock full of pine trees, with a vintage view both of Logtak lake and the surrounding villages. We were met there by the forest officials. The lake touches half the circumference of the hill and there is a forest road along the shore of the lake going full circle round the base of the hillock. We covered the circular road in about 45 minutes and came back to the guest house and settled in the open lawn in front of it, to have a closer look of the lake which spreads majestically right upto horizon on the three sides. Nungshi mentioned to me that the lake is about 50 kms long. It was difficult to approach and move about in floating islands because of the thick and tall grass. We saw them with the binoculars. The floating islands near the shore were close to each other, separated by a narrow lane of water barely few feet wide, so much so that they looked like paddy fields divided by numerous water channels. The most famous fauna, the wild boar and the deer, of these islands keep on moving from one island to the other. In fact, the celebrated 'dancing deer'—Sangai, is reported to be now surviving only in the numerous floating islands of this lake and some areas in South China. The adjective 'dancing' comes from the illusion created by the undulating movement of islands in the water caused by the movement of the animals or the wind. The conservator of Forests—who was from Karnataka, —a knowledgeable person—and an admirer of Sangai, was of the view that Sangai, originally inhabitant of the forests and hills around the lake, was driven out from there by the indiscriminate felling and burning of the forests and escaped to the safety of these islands. Safe—no doubt—but trapped forever—like the heifer engraved on the Greecian urn in Keats' famous ode. The trees and vegetation, even in their destruction, had provided shelter to Sangai, because, as per one theory, to which the Conservator of Forests also subscribed, the floating islands have been formed by the ash and charcoal of the burnt forests, washed down in to the lake by the rain through the ages. These islands are about 6 ft. thick, out of which about 3 ft. are submerged in the water. Presence of Sangai in these islands has added to the unique and pristine beauty of the lake. The Sangai float along with islands and also move from one to other as the gradual and endless process of the islands coming together and drafting apart goes on. The size of these islands ranges between less than one acre to several acres.

The lake dominates both the geography of the place and the psyche of the people. It has inspired many a folklore and is intimately linked with the joys and sorrows of its people.

After a light breakfast, we left the place. On our way back we spent some time at the INA memorial. It is a double-storied building. The first floor of the building has considerable memorabilia relating to Shri Subhash Chandra Bose and the INA. A spot in front of the building where Shri Bose had unfurled the tricolour on the Indian soil for the first time in 1943 was shown to me. A permanent iron mast now stands there on a platform and is used for hoisting the national flag on ceremonial occasions.

On the way back, I had ample time to have a good view of the endless stretch of paddy fields between the shore of the lake and the mountains.

INA Memorial and the spot where Netaji hoisted the tricolour for the first time on the Indian soil in 1943 on the outskirts of Imphal

We returned to Imphal around 10.30 am. While I was leaving the office in the evening I was informed that there was a programme of Manipuri dance later in the evening at Jawaharlal Nehru Academy of Manipur Dance, organised in honour of some official delegation which had come from Delhi. I decided to attend this programme. I had about an hour available before this programme. I therefore went to have a look at the traditional Manipuri market. The place was a square, made up of double line of single storied shops with a roof but no dividing wall between the shops. All the shops were run by the ladies. The ware consisted of handloom sarees, dupttas, blankets, Naga shawls, vegetables, fruits and other agricultural products, some of which were new to me.

It was a crowded, lively and colourful place. During the days of Kingdom, when men mostly remained busy with the perpetual wars, the ladies managed the home and also attended to agriculture and trade. Though the traditions have gradually changed, yet one can still find the ladies keeping this tradition alive gracefully. I bought a saree and dupatta after a bit of bargaining. It was not a case of price being hiked abnormally for a stranger. Bargaining was normal for everyone including the local people. One never misses the simplicity and honesty of these people even while bargaining with them. I was happy with my modest shopping.

From the market we went straight to JLN Academy of Manipuri Dance around 6 pm. The institution has the unique distinction of being one of the two central academies of dance in the country, the other being Sangeet Natak Academy at Delhi. It is located at a quiet place within the city. Apart from the office area and instruction rooms etc. it has a compact performance hall for seating a little over 100 people. The Academy was established in1954. The programme of the evening included a group dance by the ladies, sword display to the tune of mridangam, spear and sword fight, all by men, followed by group dance in Manipuri style. The martial arts display gave a glimpse of skills perfected by these people during several centuries. The display looked all the more sharp in contrast, as it followed the slower tenor of the group dance. It was given by a group of young men whose bodies seemed to have the speed of lightning and the energy of live wire. These could match the very best that the far-eastern countries have to offer. They reminded me of Chinese martial arts.

The programme was rounded off by a Raslila—'Basant Ritu'. This quintessential Manipuri classical dance performance thrilled me. I could as well be witnessing this in Mathura. One ethos binding the two extremeties of the land! As in the earlier group performance, in this also the upper body and hand movements were predominant. The leg movements, unlike in Bharatnatyam, Odissi and Kathak, are slower and invisible because of the unique costume. Instead, the effect of the entire lower body movement is reflected through rhythmic movement of the long bulbous skirt (ghagra). The most graceful part of the dance is the movement of hands which is never flat or straight but always like ripples on the surface of water or rays of light passing through transparent water ruffled by gentle breeze. They were Indian in essence but they reminded me of Thai classical dances. The young dancers, were graceful, lissom and slender and their attire, a display of rainbow colours. Between the two dances and the Raslila, the latter was swifter, with a perfect juxtaposition of hand and footwork. I could not dream of a better finale to my trip to Manipur. I kept on wondering as to how the people from the further East, may be from Thailand and Burma, during their westward journey, after crossing several mountain ranges, may have been struck by the beauty of an ancient culture, as they entered Manipur. The fragrance of the timeless mystique of India, must have been strong in this eastern extremity, which, for people coming from farther east was a threshold of India. But sadly, today it seems to be a distant, little known, misunderstood, almost a forgotten frontier, a land's end for the rest of the country. If these countrymen of ours feel neglected, discriminated and even victimized, we must sit up and find out why.

CHAPTER 11

Where the Sun Rises from the Snows

I left Imphal by 10.30 a.m. flight on December 18, 1992 and after a brief stop over at Silchar, and then over flying the hills of Silchar and the paddy fields of Bangladesh most of the way, reached Calcutta at 12.30 p.m. I could clearly make out the long thin lines formed by numerous rivers, running from North to South and two thick lines which undoubtedly were Padma and Brahmaputra while overflying Bangladesh.

I spent the rest of the day at Calcutta doing official work, the only exception being a brief visit in between, to the Customs 'tent' in the Maidan. Customs is one of the few institutions which has a plot on the outskirts of the Maidan, adjoining the hockey ground portion of it. There are several play grounds in the Maidan area. The tent has been with the department for more than hundred years. The entire vast green area surrounding these playgrounds is known as

'Maidan'. And what is termed as the Customs 'tent' is in fact a cute little cottage made of hard board and asbestos sheets, containing a bar-cum-lounge and a changing room for players and sportsmen. It has a small well-manicured lawn on the side and it faces the Maidan. No institution is allowed to have a pukka structure around the Maidan. A small path in front of it connects it directly with the play grounds of the Maidan. The 'tent' for generations now, has helped forge a bond of camaraderie and a sense of belonging among the cadres of the service and their families. On occasions like the New Year day, Puja and Diwali, get-togethers are organised in the tent. This has been the tradition, I am told, from its inception. The Central Excise too has a tent nearby.

This was my second visit to Calcutta and was as short as the first one. I was fascinated by the city and developed a tremendous liking for the city. Here, while one ruminates nostalgically about its past, still reflected in its great buildings and well preserved in its museums, one cannot also miss the decay that has set in these very structures, many of which are dilapidated and have run to seed. I am yet to have a closer look at the abject poverty and squalor which, thanks to the microscopic eye of both national and international media, are known all over the world, though there are numerous cities in India and abroad which may be equally, if not better, qualified for this dubious distinction. However, I could not miss several new features in the so-called decadent city, one such being the 6 kms long Metro. This has been built in double the number of years. The teething problems were reported to be too many, providing tonnes of ammunition to carping critics! I had also read about the flooding of the Metro tunnel sometime back during the monsoons. However, I do not recollect having read anything in newspapers in any prominent manner that this is India's first Metro. I have travelled in the metros of Hong Kong & Tokyo. Calcutta Metro, though minuscule in size, is comparable to both of them. The people of West Bengal deserve kudos for this pioneering work. This metro showed the way to others.

As I was scheduled to leave Calcutta by 12 a.m. flight next day, I decided to spend the early hrs. of the morning in Hooghly. Myself and P.N. Malhotra, a dear colleague, then Collector of Customs, Calcutta, boarded a launch early in the morning. We went down upto Garden Reach workshop and then against the current, upto new Vidya Sagar Setu. While on the move, I got a rare early morning view of the historical landmarks along the Hooghly river; the Writer's Building, the High Court, Custom House and the Mosque silhouetted against a brilliant morning sky. Job Charnock, three centuries back, may have gazed at the banks of Hooghly on several occasions while passing, when the banks might have had a different view to offer—recurring patterns of paddy fields and coconut groves in a fertile land—an endless stretch which was truly "sonar".

This set the mood for going into the shadow of the Himalayas, from "Ocean to Sky", as it were, as my next destination was Siliguri and then Gangtok via Kalimpong and finally Darjeeling. I had last breathed the Himalayan air in 1989 when I had gone to Gangotri.

We reached Siliguri around 1.30 pm. The afternoon was used up in visiting Land Customs Preventive offices along Indo-Nepal and Indo-Bangladesh borders and I had exchange of views with the two young Asstt. Collectors of Customs of the area, about the problem of smuggling across the two borders. Around 7 pm when it was totally dark, we left Siliguri for Kalimpong by jeep. I could not see anything on the way, and could hear only the loud roar of the rapid waters of Teesta, which filled the surrounding hills. We reached Kalimpong around 8. The Circuit House where I was to stay, is located away from the city at a quiet place, full of trees and at a height which gave excellent view of the lights of Kalimpong city below, about 2 kms away. The next day, as we proposed to leave early, we went to the Buddhist monastery on top of the nearby hill, just before sunrise. The monastery is small but an impressive double-storied structure. From here I got my first view of great Kanchanjanga—a towering mountain, dominating the whole area visible to the eye. Later on I realised that this was perhaps one of the two best views of this peak, the second one being from Gangtok.

We left for Gangtok at 9 am, after stopping over for a short while at Kalimpong market. It is a small but busy market, having a mix of local handicrafts and factory made goods. In olden times, Kalimpong used to be an important trading centre between India and Tibet.

We crossed over from West Bengal to Sikkim at Rangpo. The state of Sikkim starts as soon as one crosses the bridge over river Teesta at this point. One cannot miss the Pagoda-style, double-storied Government Guest House, as one crosses the bridge which signals one's entry into Sikkim. I had a distinct feeling of crossing over to a different State. The difference is perceptible in the smooth, well-kept roads, sleek new buildings, the clean and lively markets and above all, the faces of the people. The cleanliness of the inhabited area was in perfect harmony with the beauty of the nature. What is unique about the state is the typical Himalayan vegetation and air which is all pervasive from the foothills itself. Along with Himalayan vegetation, the terraced fields too can be seen from the foothills almost upto the snow-line. As we drove towards Gangtok, the road gained altitude abruptly and along the route, one could notice a variety of vegetation typical of the area, such as bamboo trees, giant yellow Cactus, Lal Patta shrubs, and 'Payun'—a kind of hill cherry which yields gum and a variety of creepers, all providing colourful contrast. Every turn of the road unfolded a similar yet different scenario. As the road winds higher, the shrubs, the creepers and the small plants give way to the pine, oak deodar and other Himalayan trees on the mountains. We came across many rivers with plentiful water, ideal for hydro-electric-projects. In fact I did notice a few such projects and quite a few industrial areas en route.

Gangtok is located at a high altitude of about 7000 ft. It becomes visible from a distance of about 10 miles from it. We reached Gangtok at 12 a.m. A room was booked for me in MLA's hostel located in a thickly wooded area, by the lower side of the road leading to the Palace. The place, though frugally furnished, was very neat and comfortable. A full view of Kanchanjanga and adjoining peaks, rising from behind the tall trees in front of building, greeted me. I could see the TV tower and some houses on top of the hill. After attending to my official work in the nearby Customs Office, I set out on foot to have the feel of the city. Excepting for M.G. market which is the main market and which is always crowded and full of life, most of the roads had few pedestrians, but plenty of vehicles, breaking the palpable silence of the place every now and then. The state and the city of Gangtok in particular, has large number of vehicles and taxies. The transport system seems to be excellent. While men wore dresses common elsewhere in the country, ladies wore both traditional Sikkimese long skirts or gowns as well as salwar-kameez, sarees, skirts and jeans etc. The markets and the roads were very clean. Many new multi storied cement structures had sprung up in recent years. However, these are but few odd spots in the overwhelming greenery of the area which is still unspoiled. Even during a short interface with the people, normally reticent to the outsiders, one cannot miss their simplicity and forthrightness.

After strolling in the MG market and the nearby roads, the palace of the erstwhile Chogyal was my next destination. It is located on top of the hillock which, not so long ago when the city had not spread out to the surrounding heights, might have been the highest point of the city. It is comparably small structure for a palace, a two-storied building, now guarded by CRPF jawans. It is now uninhabited and is closed for public. It has a Pagoda-style top with yellow painted roof. One gets the best view of the entire Gangtok, the Himalayas, Nathu La Pass and perhaps the entire state from the Palace.

I spent about 45 minutes in the palace compound and walked back to the hostel, with some disappointment at not having been able to take the photographs of the Palace, as photography is prohibited there.

Early next morning we started for the Snow-view—the highest point of Gangtok city located about 6 kms away on top of the hill towards the north. The sky was clear and we reached the spot just as the sun was rising, from the distant steel-grey, Himalayan peaks in the eastern horizon. And right in front, with nothing between us, stood the majestic peak of Kanchanjanga in its morning splendour. This perhaps was the most proximate and the best view of a Himalayan peak that I had so far seen. The only other place where I get similar feeling of proximity is Kausani in Almora. And when I turned my gaze towards Gangtok, I got another unique view, this time of Gangtok city from a higher level. Even from this distance, one cannot miss the solitary yellow Palace building, being the only structure in that hillock covered by trees for considerable distance beyond its grounds. The Palace, being atop the hill, is in fact visible from nearly every point in the city. It overlooks and dominates the city in the same way as Kanchanjanga dominates everything upto the the horizon and is visible to the naked eye from this point. I took the photographs of the palace—a tiny but clear yellow spot from that distance, though.

We left for Darjeeling at 1 p.m. As we were advised to reach before dark, in view of the tense situation caused by a political murder in the city, we took a short cut which passes through the tea gardens on the northern face or the shadow side of the Darjeeling hills. The road was rather narrow and mostly used by the people of tea gardens. It was an immensely enjoyable drive. Darjeeling was a transit place for me with just a few hours of next morning available to me to see the place before I left for Siliguri. I therefore decided to go to Tiger Hill next morning to see the sun-rise and follow it up by a quick stroll through the city. We reached Darjeeling around 6 pm. I stayed in the new circuit house. The first floor room allotted to me gave an excellent view of the city and a few Himalayan peaks.

Next morning I got up at 3.30 am and set out for the Tiger Hill at 4 am along with the local Customs Officer. It was a steep uphill drive of about 10 kms. It was pitch dark. We overtook many groups of people including women and children who were making it on foot towards the Tiger Hill. We reached the Tiger Hill top at 4.45 am. The place was already crowded with hundreds of people standing on the ground, around the two storied watch—tower. I got a ticket entitling me to a standing place on the first floor of the watch tower. It was still so dark that one could hardly make out the faces of the people even a meter away as the place had no electricity. The people were jostling around in the din. I however distinctly remember the faces of two young boys in their teens. I had a glimpse of their faces when one of them lit a cigarette. And in that momentary flash I saw the youthful and ecstatic glow in their faces. They had a small rucksack on their backs and one of them was wearing a canvass hat. After a while they started singing a Nepali song and danced in slow graceful movements. They sang and danced with complete abandon for about 10 minutes. The rest of the crowd took hardly any notice of them. I asked my Nepali driver about the meaning of the song. He explained that the refrain of the song said that they had come from Gangtok which is a beautiful place. Perhaps one of the most beautiful sights of nature—the breaking of the dawn, had filled them with ecstasy which burst out from within them in to that song and dance. The sun rose at 6 am from the distant ranges of the Himalayas in Bhutan and Arunachal Pradesh, in the east, which appeared steel-grey, rather than golden red, because of faint mist. I strained my eyes to see Mount Everest towards the north, expecting that the first golden rays of the rising sun would fall on its peak and illuminate it. However, the mist in that area had shrouded the peak too. The crowd, after witnessing the scenario for about 15 minutes, started dispersing in groups, some viewing the other ranges from different spots. I tried to locate the young singers from Gangtok. I could not locate them. May be they were very near to me but they had merged in the crowd. Their song however continued to linger in my mind for a long time. My regret at missing the view of Mount Everest at sunrise, was partially set off when the Customs Officer promised to procure a copy of the photograph of the peak taken by his friend in Darjeeling, who was a professional photographer and had a life-long fascination for the majestic peak. He kept his promise. His photographer friend had succeeded in capturing the grandeur of the south face of Mount Everest, resplendent in the golden rays of sunrise.

As the sunlight flooded the area, it dissipated the magic of the dawn. After about another 15 minutes, as soon as the sun had half emerged from the mountains and turned the Himalayan ranges near and far into gold, I left the place

Band Stand, Darjeeling

and came back to the circuit house. After a wash, I hurried out for a stroll in the main road of this hill station, which is mostly even, without any sharp ups and downs. There were hardly any people on the road as it was still early. I walked up to Raj Bhawan about three kms away. On my way back I stopped at the Band Stand for about 15 minutes. This forms one end of the market, a relic of the British times. There is an open circular space here with shops constructed over the 3/4th of the circle. These are old style buildings mostly single storied and having sloping roofs covered with red corrugated tin sheets. They were beautiful. On my way back, after taking a snap of the city and the old Municipality building with clock tower, I left the city of Darjeeling with some regret. The filth and lack of sanitation had all but marred its beauty. But the decadence of the man made city cannot yet overshadow the abundance of its natural beauty, exotic flora and fauna, and the breathtaking view of the Himalayas.

In fact Himalayas alone make all the difference: One giant range, with a thousand lofty peaks, from Kashmir to Arunachal, the biggest in the world, a colossus casting its benign shadow over India's history and geography for thousands of years, an object of shared experience, generating a feeling of awe, admiration, love and perhaps reverence in a billion people, as much a reflection as a Creator of its ethos!

CHAPTER 12

Calcutta, 2008-09 Getting to know Calcutta and Tagore as a Child

CALCUTTA for me is associated with the memories of my schooldays, when I was learning the rudiments of English. This started rather late, well after I had passed out of primary school. That is how the educational system of the state was at that time. In fact the real introduction with the language and its grammar did not start till I had reached 9th standard.

The first ever school which I attended as a child at the age of about four was 'Adam's' in Almora city, now part of Uttarakhand state. Many in the city preferred to call it just 'Mission School', finding the word 'Missionary ' perhaps too tongue twisting. And contrary to the impression that the name 'Adam's 'might convey to an outsider, and despite its administrator at that time being one Miss Cox, perhaps a

British lady, it was neither an English medium school nor a public school but a Hindi medium school under U.P. Board. In fact, the city did not have any public or English medium school, in contrast to nearby Nainital which could boast of schools like St George's and Sherwood. Adam's had co-education upto the 5th standard and was a girls' school from the 6th to the 10th standards! I spent three years in that school, from nursery to the 2nd standard. Nursery was all play. Ms S. Singh was our clsss teacher for the 1st standard and Ms G. Singh for 2nd. I got my grounding of Hindi alphabets, numbers, additions, subtractions, multiplication tables etc., in those three years. I have fond memories of this school which is located at a beautiful spot on the eastern brow of the long ridge, atop and on both sides of which Almora city is built. Its sloping and spacious compound, buildings at different levels, and wooded environs set it apart from the rest of the schools in the city.

My initiation to English, in accordance with U.P. Board system, came only in the 6th standard by which time I had left Adam's and moved to Govt Model School which was known as Middle School i.e., upto 8th standard. There in the 6th standard, we were taught to write English alphabets in ink with 'G' nib, fixed in a holder. It helped everyone except me to evolve a beautiful hand writing. This was followed by reading and writing of some simple words and sentences.and learning the rudiments of grammar. I fared comparatively better here. I have fond memories of this school too. This was located at lower levels of the western face of Almora's long ridge. Its several buildings too were located at different levels of the slope. The whole area was quite shaded, with a variety of sub-Himalayan trees, including some Deodars in its compound. The teachers those days, not lured by the culture of private coaching, widely prevalent today, were sincerely committed to give their best to the pupil. They were strict disciplinarians. I still remember, how a rare slip on my part, when I forgot to do my maths homework, earned me six lusty lashes on each palm by a cane from my class teacher in the 7th, Shri Narayan Singh. Apart from another habitual defaulter, I was the only one to get that punishment that day. My palms turned red and were burning till late in the evening. I never defaulted thereafter. After passing the 8th, and primed with rudimentary knowledge of English, I joined the 9th standard in Ramsey Inter College, another 'Mission' school in the city, for doing my matriculation i.e., the 9th and the 10th standards. Lest anyone had any lurking doubt about the standard of teaching in general and English in particular in that school, the school staff, never missed an opportunity to mention, with considerable gusto and pride, that Shri Govind Ballabh Pant was an alumnus of Ramsey. Shri Pant had gone on to become a brilliant and perhaps the most prominent lawyer of the region. What followed after that is history. It is difficult to gauge how much Ramsey school had helped Shri Pant to master and hone his English, or contributed to his legal acumen. But in all likelihood, it was here that he had picked up the rudiments of an alien language. For me, one of the vivid memories of the school is the daily reading of a couple of pages from the Hindi Bible, by the Principal in the morning assembly, touching upon the anecdotes of Jesus Christ's life. They were absorbing stories, and I have not forgotten most of them since then. It was only much later when I read the English Bible, that I discovered how these anecdotes have been clothed in simple words and pithy sentences which have a timeless beauty, and which never fail to make a profound impression on the reader.

Two English text-books were prescribed for High School classes. They were a collection of half a dozen short pieces in prose by English and Indian writers, and a collection of about ten poems of one page or less, with two or three stanzas, each. The poets were, Wordsworth, Longfellow, Blake, Thomas Carew and some others. The prose pieces were by Nehru, Gandhi, Tagore, A.G. Gardiner and some others. The piece by Tagore was an autobiographical one extracted perhaps from one of his several autobiographical writings. The piece started somewhat like this:

"The Calcutta where I was born ..."

And it went on to describe the Calcutta of his childhood.

Our teacher was at pains to explain why the writer had used the article 'The' before 'Calcutta 'which was a proper noun. My teacher spoke his English haltingly, interspersing every word or sentence of English with several words or sentences in Hindi. That was the way he could teach and that was the only way that the students could follow him. And as he explained to us the piece by Tagore, we listened with rapt attention. Tagore's description of Calcutta of his childhood cast a spell on me. Much later, when I read Gandhiji, I realized that Shri Tagore had echoed or perhaps presaged Gandhiji, when he said in this piece that the city dwellers, who sped past the villages in their cars 'at sixty miles an hour', could know little about real India. Gandhiji believed that the soul of India lived in the villages. Some more details of that Calcutta of yore were given by him there. This was the city which was the capital of British India when it was at its zenith, till the capital was shifted to Delhi. It must have been a grand and sprawling city. And since those early days, I always fancied a visit to the city and have a close look at it and find what remained of that 'Calcutta' of Tagore in today's Kolkata. It was also my fervent desire, right from that time, to read the entire works of Tagore. The former part of this desire was finally realized in 2008-09. The latter, to my regret, remains partially fulfilled. But I have not given up yet.

Visiting Calcutta as a Grownup—a Closer Look at the City and Some of Its Historical Personages

I visited Calcutta for the first time in1981, and did not miss the, grandeur of Calcutta of old. The process of decadence that perhaps had set in after the capital shifted to

Delhi, was as unmistakable to me as was its grandeur, even though I passed through its streets, mostly on official errands "at sixty miles an hour"in a speeding car. This was a fleeting visit. My several subsequent visits to the city between 1992 and 2002 were all official and not much different from the first one. Moving from one office to another for meetings and discussions, left little time for a closer look at the roads, buildings and monuments of the city. But in the late nineties, I noticed a perceptible change. Something rare, which does not normally happen, at least in India, had happened to the city. Decadence had either been checked or slowed down. The traffic was one way in most of the business area and moved more smoothly. Roads were better maintained and cleaner. I managed to have at least a cursory look at some of its interesting landmarks like Park St, Strand Road, Dalhousie Square, Belur Math, with Swami Vivekananda's room in it overlooking Hooghly, Maidan and the Customs and Central Excise 'tents' in it.

End of 2007 brought me to 'Calcutta' again, long after my retirement in 2002. I was there for the whole of 2008 in several spells, ranging from 20 days to two months, respectively. And I left it at end of January 2009. These visits were very enjoyable as I had not come officially but as a common visitor to the city, with a relaxed mind and had all the time in the world at my disposal.

It was my daughter Shubhra's transfer to Calcutta in 2007, that brought us to the city this time. Our grand daughter, who was two and half years old at that time, needed to be looked after, when my daughter was away to the office all day. We volunteered to do that and found ourselves at Kolkata.

We and her mother in-law decided to be with her by turns. It was a most enjoyable chore. This also helped me to make up for what I had missed when my children were growing up. That time was the early part of my career. The demands of my assignments at that time did not leave as much time for the family and children as I would have wished. But now I had plenty of time for my grand-daughter. There is no experience like watching a child grow. And I had seen her from the day of her birth, when her eyes had that swollen look, and were closed for a couple days, and an angelic and mysterious smile gently played on her face every now and then. I used to wonder what dreams or thoughts could be generating those smiles. And then one day, she uttered her first syllable when she was about three months old, started talking and walking when she was eight months old and gradually thereafter, started asking those innocent questions, arising out of the unlimited curiosity of a child. Calcutta was a continuation of this. She kept us busy all day. But I had free time during my morning walks and the weekends, when my daughter was at home. I decided to have a look at the city during my free time, including the morning walks, not with a microscope, but with reading glasses, just close enough not to miss any interesting detail and distant enough so as not to get lost in details. I did not want to miss the woods for the trees. I was curious to find how much of old Calcutta of Rabindra Nath Tagore's boyhood, and Calcutta preceding and following it, till the capital shifted to Delhi, had survived in the present day Kolkata. It was heartening to find that Calcutta was not dead and all history, but alive in many ways. In the process, I not only saw a bit of both but experienced much more. A lingering feeling has however remained with me that one year was too short a period for a city with so much past, which has a live link to its present. Its museum alone required a couple of months to have a proper look at its treasures.

I wanted to read some book on 'Calcutta' as a prelude before I set about to see the city. I asked my daughter to get me some book on the city from her office library. From the limited choice available, I selected a book titled "Echoes From Old Calcutta" by H.E. Busteed. Its sub title was 'Reminiscences of the days of Warren Hastings, Frances and Impey.'

The book did not have the type of information that I was

looking for. But it did have a captivating account of some prominent English men of eighteenth century, all of whom were important players in the history of that era. And actions of one of them viz. Warren Hastings played pivotal role in shaping the future course of Indian history. And in that process, the face of Calcutta too changed. He was in India earlier too for a short stint. But what turned out to be momentous historically, was his second stint of thirteen years, from 1772 to 1785 when he joined as Governor of Bengal. The author himself considers him to be the greatest Briton of the eighteenth century. Not all may agree with this assessment. But few would disagree that he was one of the most remarkable men of his age. I do not wish to dwell in detail on the historical facts contained in the book, or their historical value, both being beyond my competence. But before cutting off this digression, I wish to briefly touch upon a couple of aspects of the book which, hopefully, at least some, if not all, readers may find interesting.

Hastings emerges from these pages as an outstanding administrator; who kept his aplomb even in the gravest of crisis. Despite occupying a powerful position, he was modest in his demeanour, and not given to public display of his immense power and authority. The trappings of the high office were kept to the minimum. And his letters to Mrs. Hastings, written while he or she was away from Calcutta, mostly to a friend's place in Chinsura, north of Calcutta on the Hoogly, reflect a very thoughtful loving and caring husband, doting but never excessively.

The other aspect relates to the trial and execution of Raja Nand Kumar and the English attack, led personally by Hastings himself, on Raja Chait Singh of Benares. Quite a bit has been written about these two events in the Indian history books. But what Busteed, an admirer of Hastings, has to say about them, makes an interesting reading. It goes thus.

"Nun Coomar " was Governor of Hooghly in 'Siraj-ud-daulah's' time. Title of Maharajah was conferred on him by Emperor Shah Alam in 1764. He was one of the most influential men of his time in Bengal, or perhaps most influential after the Nawab in Bengal. The cause of Hastings' prejudice against Nand Kumar is a matter of speculation. The author does not throw any light on this. Perhaps Hastings did not find him favourably inclined or cooperative enough towards him, and thus an impediment in his path. And when an appropriate occasion arose he was charged rather dubiously, but in accordance with due process of law, as it existed then. It was a trial by jury.

As seen from the copy of the warrant issued, the two trial judges wrote to "Sheriff of the Town of Calcutta and Factory of Fort William in Bengal and to the Keeper of His Majesty's prison at Calcutta" to receive "body of Maharajah Nuncoomar"—"charged before us—with feloniously uttering as true a false and counterfeit writing obligatory, knowing the same to be false and counterfeit, in order to defraud the executors of Bolaukee Doss, deceased."

"The bond and deed which the accused was charged with uttering, knowing it to be forged, purported to be the acknowledgement of a debt to him from a native shroff or banker incurred several years before. This was settled by executioners. (Rs. 70, 000.00 plus some other amount about their substance)."

Put simply the charge against Nand Kumar was that he had fabricated a document which showed that "Bolaukee Doss" had taken a loan of Rs 70000.00 plus some other amount which was settled by the executioners of the latter's will after his death. The punishment for forgery at that time was death! And the charge was proved.

There was denial of natural justice as the counsel of charged person (Nand Kumar) was not allowed to address the jury. Nand kumar had his own witnesses to prove that the bond was genuine.

The advocate for Nand Kumar sought permission of the

Chief Justice Impey to petition the jury to recommend the case of his client to the King for mercy. He cited a precedent for this. It appears that while putting the request to the Chief Justice he had referred to his client as "unhappy victim". The response of the Chief Justice, to quote the author, was:

"Chief Justice (Impey) administered to him a severe reprimand and told him his conduct was derogatory to his professional character, that no advocate in England, who had proper regard for the dignity of the court would have so acted. Juries must be protected from improper application to them. What did he mean by "unhappy victim?"

The advocate, according to the author, gave some explanation. The matter ended there. Nand Kumar was executed by hanging.

This certainly is not how a judicial mind functions. Given the long history of English judicial system, no judge, unless he was biased or had allowed himself to be influenced, would have acted the way Chief Justice Impey did. Though the author does not say it in so many words, one cannot but get the impression that the chief Justice had been influenced, directly or indirectly, by Warren Hastings. As the matter involved dealing with the judicial system and the judicial process, the executive power had to be used discreetly by Hastings. The author's language is unmistakably defensive in dealing with this issue. One has, however, to give credit to the British political system, as impeachment proceedings were initiated against Hastings, his invaluable contribution to the empire notwithstanding, and Impey. And pitted against them was one of the greatest British parliamentarians of all times, Sir Edmund Burke. One of the articles of impeachment for Impey read:

> "There is certainly a great improbability that a man of Nuncoomar's rank and fortune should be guilty of so mean an offence for so small a sum of money."

The stain of this trial has never been washed from British hands and remains there for perpetuity. But one has to admire the British judicial system. When the all powerful governor general wanted to act in breach of it, he did so by taking every care to ensure that he appeared to be working within the system. No one was above it. And when Hastings was found culpable, he had to be answerable too.

In the case of Chait Singh he did not have to be discreet. Here he was not fettered by British judicial system, as he was in the case of Nand Kumar. Hastings had more freedom here and he used it to the full. That called for courage though. Expansion of His Majesty's empire was a most worthy cause. For this worthy end the means did not matter, even if it meant annihilation of a tiny and hapless state.

"Hastings had decided to go personally to Benares as Chait Singh had for sometime failed to comply with increasing demand for extra-ordinary tributes made on him by the Company's Govt to help in defraying the war expense."

Going by the choice of words, it is seen that the author has been honest about the brashness of the demand and the strong-arm tactics resorted to by Hastings.

Hastings came to Benares in August 1781. He occupied a detached building called "Mahadur Dass Garden house". Hastings sought to arrest Chait Singh on 14.8.1781 at Ramnagar. The Rajah however escaped to Lateefpur. Hastings' assault on Ramnagar thus failed. Fearing an attack by the hostile forces, he withdrew to Chunar next morning with four hundred sepoys. There seems to have been some sort of a rout. He returned to Benares on 28.9.1781 to accomplish the aborted mission, after additional forces came.

The people of Benares, who had witnessed this event have left a two line limerick in Hindi for the posterity. The author has quoted it in the book. It runs:

> "*Ghore par howdah, hathi per zeen,*
> *Jeldi bhag gaya, Warren Hasteen.*"

Its free translation would be that Warren Hastings ran away (from Benares), in such haste, that the zeen, meant to be strapped on a horse, was put on the elephant, and 'howdah' meant to be strapped on the elephant, was put on the horse!

While it was Warren Hastings, who had the last laugh in the matter, the people of Benares, at least at that time when the limerick was composed, must have thought that they had got even with the mighty Englishman!

Amongst the letters of Hastings to his wife, there is one from Chunar dated 8.9.1781. While concluding the letter he says. "This is climate of paradise". This was the climate of the Gangetic plains, in fact the whole of the north in mid-September about two hundred and fifty years back. After the oppressive heat of the Indian summer, and the unbearable mugginess of July and August, September indeed was the beginning of a heavenly climate. And it used to be like this as late as twenty years back. But there has been perceptible change in climate since then. Uncharacteristically, summer months, for some years now, have been having many intermittent showers thus taking the sting out of the dreaded summer. But according to many old timers, this has also taken away the deliciousness and sweetness of many a summer fruit like melon, mangoes etc. Nature has been even handed in dealing out its favours –giving some and taking away some! And the heat and humidity which used to die out by middle of September, now extend well beyond, almost by a month. Climate change has come to stay! And the global warming, closing in so menacingly, may further change even the present climate for the worse.

The City with a Soul—Its Tram, Streets, Shops, Markets, Buildings, Pavement Dwellers, Its Parks and Cultural Milieu

My daughter was allotted an official accommodation in the central govt flats in Nizam Palace, which is located at A.J.C. Bose Road, a central location in the city. The old Nizam Palace from which the area gets its name, is a heritage building now, and is being used as a central govt office. It is a three storied ornate building of European design painted in white. The vintage building looks elegant. Several multistoried office buildings, and two multistoried residential complexes have come behind it in the sprawling compound. The rear gate of the compound, close to the residential complex, leads to Lee Road where several new multistoried buildings, with multiplexes, shopping complexes, Big Bazar, car park and immensely popular Forum Mall etc. have come up in recent times.

During my several visits to the city in 2008-2009, I started walking the streets of Calcutta, something which I could not do during my earlier visits. As I moved about in a leisurely pace, with a relatively free mind now, I felt that I was not a stranger or an outsider, but belonged here always. The mega city seemed to have, what most of the modern cities, and certainly all big ones lack –a soul, and a benign one at that. And it manifests itself in various ways, as I was to discover gradually. Its life has a relaxed pace, and therefore a newcomer is not swept off his feet by its speed, as happens in other big cities. As the city gets modernized, the pace of its life is bound to accelerate. One only wishes that the acceleration is not too much to make it lose its character. And the city shelters everyone, no matter from where one comes, near or far, Bengali or non-Bengali alike, and it rarely fails to do its bit so that each one of its denizens not only survives, but does so with at least a modicum of dignity.

Even if someone gives away his identity by his language, accent, and demeanour as a newcomer to the city and as an outsider, one is not made conscious of it or taken notice of, which is different from being ignored. When a Bengali, and certainly one with even a modicum of education, instead of plainly saying that he comes from such a village, city or locality, says, instinctively, prompted by his 'sanskars' and upbringing, that he is a "Bhalo Bashi" of a particular place, he is not indulging in self praise or displaying a sense of superiority, or making a tall claim. It only means that he puts store by being a good citizen and he can be trusted and taken for his word. It is more a statement of intent. If the intent is sincere, something of it always translates into reality. And it is manifest in its people from even the humblest of background, whether in the cities or villages. Veneer of that culture, howsoever thin, Indian in spirit and ethos and typically Bengali in some of its manifestations, is present in every one. Acceptance of outsiders, and tolerance for them, perhaps became part of their heritage, and tradition as they have been familiar with outsiders for several centuries now. Nearby Murshidabad was the seat of Mughal Governors and Calcutta was the capital of the British during most of their rule. Therefore people from different parts of the country had been gravitating to it for ages. They are passionate about their heritage and culture, inviting at times the uncharitable accusation of subnationalism. This may not be going down well with many of them, when so many from the earlier generations had been at the forefront of freedom struggle from its very inception. The nationalist and pan-Indian credentials of these freedom fighters were beyond doubt. The only blemish or wart in this otherwise 'Bhalo Bashi' portrait is an occasional tendency to take law into their own hands, perhaps out of a sense of outrage, in cases where someone appears to have been responsible for a traffic accident or injury. They have to be wary here, even if such incidents are mere aberrations.

The unique kaleidoscope of cultures and traditions of different states and regions that is India, this colourful fabric, this tapestery which is a riot of so many hues and patterns, which makes India unique, will lose its character and cease to exist, unless each one of them is carefully nurtured and preserved. Perhaps everyone would be loath to see this unique fabric getting torn and disintegrated. Then why accuse anyone of sub-nationalism? As historian Ramchandra Guha makes the interesting point, the Indian and American societies, both great in their own ways, make for an interesting study in contrast. The former has assimilated different cultures without any conflict and the latter has preserved its numerous shades, colours and patterns, also without conflict, some aberrations, both past and present excepted. But no one, who has grown up with the latter, would like to see a dull and monotonous amalgam of all cultures to emerge, where identity of each one is lost in it. Preserving the variety of our culture calls for some discipline. When each is unique, then each must have a heart to accept the others too to be so. Problems arise when one claims superiority over others. What must be shunned, is being abrasive in these matters, as otherwise genuine pride in one's culture or unique heritage, is likely to be mistaken as an attempt to look down upon others or to claim supreriority. It may be difficult to preserve one's culture without taking pride in it. And one cannot think of preserving and nurturing one's language except by speaking and writing it. If that be sub nationalism, then so be it. But such an accusation is rather unfair for a people, who have been eclectic, and produced some of the finest exponents of Hindustani classical music, vocal and instrumental alike.

For sustaining our diversity, in all its colours and shades, it is essential that the unique traditions and culture of each state or region or even district are reared and preserved with a sense of pride. One must however keep one's windows open to let the fresh air in. And one need not be frightened of the diversity because an invisible, imperceptible and undefinable thread, one could perhaps call it Indianness, a unique ethos, cutting across every barrier, binds them all together.

One of the first streets of Calcutta that I walked, lay between the rear boundary of Nizam Palace, and Forum Mall. It can be accessed through the rear gate of Nizam Palace compound. Though veering away from the Lee Road towards Sarat Bose Road, it is still known as Lee Road in this stretch. As I came out of the gate and walking to the left reached the Mother Dairy booth, I saw a signboard fixed on an iron pole put up by KMC (Kolkata Municipal Corporation), which read,

"Senior Citizens Are Our Assets, Respect Them". Though it read like an exhortation, which should have more appropriately found place in the roads of Delhi, it was, as I realized gradually during my stay in the city, part of the city's ethos. I was elated and touched to find that a city, so far off from my own, has put value on my grey hairs! And I had no doubt that should I or any other senior citizen, require any assistance, half a dozen people would rush to offer it. And the city cared for its women and children no less. This was a far cry from Delhi, which, as is evident from frequent newspaper and media reports about eve-teasing, molestation, kidnapping, ransom, assault and murder etc. is rude, brutal and inhuman to its children, many a time of tender age, senior citizens and women. No shame can be greater for a city which boasts itself to be the capital of India. One cannot put the entire blame for this, as is invariably done, on law and order machinery and the administration. They no doubt need to be strengthened and modernized considerably. They can make a difference, but cannot by themselves eliminate this evil. At the root of this are the people themselves. And they therefore are the ultimate remedy too. The upbringing and ambience must change their mind-set. And those who are well-meaning, should cease to be just helpless onlookers, resigned to suffer what they consider only as a law and order problem, to be solved by the system or the administration and police. The home and school have an important role to play at the formative stage. People have to reject this culture of violence against the vulnerable and week, and must show courage to fight when they witness it. One of the most important factors that defines the quality and character of a modern city, is the safety of its citizens, particularly its children, women and elderly. Perhaps no city is as safe as Calcutta for them. It is a soothing and reassuring sight to see women and children moving without fear or hesitation in its strees even in odd hours. What happened in Rabindra Sadan, or perhaps at Rabindra Sarobar, some decades back, or occasional news about robbery at senior citizens' place or, some case of molestation etc., is like a news from some other planet, a mere aberration. It would be pity if this city loses its ethos.

A few steps further on the road, there was a black board on the wall, big enough for spreading three or four pages of at least two newspapers While passing by, one could notice Hindi and Bengali newspapers pasted on it, though not regularly. A small signboard on top of it, indicated that it was sponsored by "Lion's Club of Calcutta, Paradise". And many passers-by, mostly vendors, construction workers, labourers and rickshaw pullers, did stop by the board and read the newpapers.

During my subsequent walks, I discovered two more boards, fixed high on electric poles near Elgin Road crossing on the Chowranghee Road. These were put up by KMC (Kolkota Municipal Corporation) and K.P. (Kolkota Police). They read:

"Respect your Culture"

and

"Nation comes before caste, colour and creed"

That word 'Nation'in the latter seemed to have a far off and unreal ring, when in recent times, the country has witnessed so much of paranoia about the primacy of local interests, even if they hurt others grievously and ran counter to concept of one nation. KMC and Kolkata police deserve to be complimented.

For about a month initially we stayed in a second floor flat near Park Circus, overlooking the main road and tram track till my daughter got a regular govt accommodation. Two tram routes originated from nearby Gariahat, one going to Chowranghee, and the other to Howrah Bridge, via Burra Bazar, passing through a sea of humanity and a jungle of multistoried buildings, some modern but mostly of late nineteenth century or early twentieth century vintage, with strong touch of English architecture. The tram network of the city is quite impressive, covering all important markets and localities. It gives choice of a cheap and efficient transport to city dwellers particularly to working and poor classes. But the condition of the couches and tracks leaves much to be desired. Little, or not enough seems to have been done to renovate or spruce up this invaluable asset, after the British left six decades back. But amazingly, the system seems to work. It is a different matter that the amalgam of clinking, rattling and grinding din emanating from the moving tram, is more deafening than the noise made by half a dozen road-rollers if made to move in tandem. The tram has two coaches, the front one being first class and the rear one, second. Despite my sincere attempt, I could not find any apparent difference between the two classes, excepting that, the first class was in the front, and less crowded, possibly because it carried a higher fare. Calcutta is the only city in the country where the tram system has survived. For this the credit goes to Calcuttans who, while not allowing it to die, have managed to keep it in a suspended animation. The system can still be renovated and turned into remarkable public transport system. Its entire infrastructure, though in bad shape, is still intact. The state would do well to preserve and restore it to its original glory. Laying of new tram lines in modern cities does not appear to be a viable proposition. It is therefore a prized possession of any city which already has one. Hong Kong, San Francisco, Vienna, Christ Church, and Budapest, each have a tram system unique in its own way and reminiscent of an old world charm. They add a new dimension to the city life, and are a great tourist attraction. Calcutta trams are waiting to be lifted to that level.

It was December 2007. We had just come to Calcutta. My grand-daughter was very keen to have a tram ride. As she was to join a play school only in March next, day time was free for me for a tram ride. I took her out thrice for tram ride around 11 a.m., by which time the office rush was nearly over. The first trip was to Gariahat and back, with one way ticket of Rs. 2 only. Being short trip, it was over within an hour. She was simply thrilled. She wanted to have more trips. I therefore took her on two more occasions, for longer trips to Chowranghee and Howrah Bridge respectively. On both the occasions, one way ticket cost a princely sum of Rs 4! I wondered if any other city in the world offered such a cheap transport. Shreya, my grand-daughter, sat on my lap, facing the window on both the occasions. The round trips covering a distance of about 15 kilometers, took about two hours.

On both these occasions, I passed through the heart of Calcutta and had a closer look at its streets and buildings. Those buildings, more than hundred years or even older, seemed desperate to prolong their existence into future as much as possible. Some had already given way to swanky new buildings. Many streets and buildings still carried their English names.

Whenever any man or lady, no matter what his age was, passed by our seat, while getting in or out of the tram, he or she invariably had a smile and a few affectionate words in Bengali or occasionally in English for my grand-daughter. The city doted on its kids. My grand-daughter kept on looking at the constantly changing scenario outside the window, with wide-eyed wonder. At the terminal points, I got down on both the occasions, and holding her hand, walked around the busy area for sometime, before boarding the tram again to go back home. And this time, her curiosity having already been quenched, she was lulled to sleep by the din and vibrations of the moving tram. I woke her up when we were about to get down. And when we reached home, she had plenty to tell about her adventure for many days. Her excitement in relating her adventure, never diminished.

I invariably got up around 4.30 a.m. and switched on FM radio, 'Big' 92.5 or occasionally 96.7 band. Brushing, shaving and breathing and bending exercises were completed in the next one and half hours, to the tune of soulful Bengali and Hindi devotional and other music rendered by various singers. Sometimes there were compositions of Tagore too. Some of the numbers like 'He Chamunde' 'Nando Kumar Khele Holi' 'Kusume Kusume Charon Chinho Diye' and 'Aiso Saimalo Sundaro—Baje Re Konkono, Baje Re Kinkini' continue to echo in my memory as much for the beauty of their language as for the quality of their music. 'Aiso Saimolo Sundaro ' was simply enchanting. I was keen to know the name of the singer and buy this C.D. The knowledgeable lady incharge in Music World, to whom I was referred, surprised me by telling that it was a song of Tagore and the singer was Asha Bhonsle and then promptly produced the CD containing this and many other songs. I was amazed by the authenticity of the singer's Bengali pronounciation. I was however not convinced, though the lady must be correct, when, in resoponse to my query, she told me that 'Eso Shyamalo Sundaro' referred to dark clouds, and not Krishna, as was my impression. Ajoy Ckakraborty's 'He Chamunde' rendered with considerable feeling was also one of my favourites. I was keen to buy this CD too. But no music store, surprisingly even Music World in Park St or the shops at Dharamtala had it. The Music World noted my request in their thick register kept for the purpose. But I am still waiting for a call from them. In fact I have never got a call from any music shop for any of my requests, despite the requests being diligently noted in a big register! I have not tested Alurkar and Rhythm House at Pune and Mumbai, respectively so far, both known for their rich repertoire of Indian classical music, though I have visited them a few times.

Normally I set out for my morning walk around 6 am after taking my favourite ginger and tulsi tea, which I prepared myself. It was Victoria Park area which was most frequented by me. For this, I walked out of the Nizam Palace compound to AJC. Bose Road, and turning left, walking along the flyover, went either to the Citizen's Park, or Peace Park or walking along the Cathedral Road towards Birla Planetoriam and Park St, went to Elliot's Park, opposite Tata Steel building. All the three parks are part of the vast expanse of open and green land called Maidan. As one comes out of the congested city to this lush green vastness, one is transported to a different world. The first two parks have been carved out of the large grounds on the left side of the Victoria Memorial. A boundry wall now separates them from the memorial.

The first one, the smallest of the three, is Peace Park, nearest to the rear entrance of the memorial. It is roundish in shape, with paved walkways going around and across it. It has a variety of shrubs and flower plants, but its distinguishing features to me were its heavy wrought-iron benches and neatly painted, clean and small rectangular boards, also with ornate frame, welded on a solid iron rod, embedded on the ground at several points along the walk way. Someone from the K.M.C. had, selected the quotes from thesaurus and reproduced on these boards. Such a gesture from the state or a public institution, may be suspect for some and may militate against freedom of choice in a democracy for some others. But these were apolitical and thought provoking quotes. And the choice of reading or not reading them, or reading and then ignoring or rejecting rested with the reader. The mind is most receptive and fresh in the mornings before one is overtaken by the worries of the day. I could not but compliment the unknown official of the corporation, for this initiative, so uncharacteristic of a bureaucrat. I made my own choice, though I liked most of the quotes and memorised the following from the lot:

> "Concentrate all your thoughts on the task at hand.
> The sun's rays do not burn until brought to a focus."
>
> —*Alaxander Graham Bell*

> "A happy heart makes a cheerful face."

> "Keep your eyes on the stars and feet on the ground."
>
> —*Theodore Roosevelt*

"That man is the richest, whose pleasures are the cheapest."

—*Henry David Thoreau*

"There is no true greatness, where there is no simplicity."

—*Leo Tolstoy*

"Am I not destroying my enemies when I make friends with them?"

—*Abraham Lincoln*

Next to the Peace Park is the Citizen's Park separated from it by an intersecting road, rectangular and longish, and divided into two by another intersecting road, leading to the left entrance of the memorial. Both these parks have a variety of flowering plants, shrubs, and hedges. But what I liked most, were the the lotus flowers in the small pond at the end of the park. The park provides a good view of the tower of St Paul's cathedral and Tata Steel building which dominates the skyline. I had a memorable experience in the park one morning. I saw a vulture perched on the tallest tree in the park, with a group of crows, sitting in several branches around it, some fluttering over it every now and then, as if to tease and chase it away. It was a rare sight, as vultures, simply disappeared ten years back from the entire north, from Rajasthan to West Bengal. The situation in the southern states may not be different either. I perhaps saw the same vulture on top of the same tree again after a few days. I wish this is a definite sign of revival of this bird, an indispensable scavenger of nature, which, many had come to believe, was extinct, at least in India.

A broad road going towards the front side of the memorial, separates this park from the Elliot's Park, which is much bigger in width and length than the other parks. It has a variety of big trees, a big pond with fountains, and spacious lawns. Its main entrance is opposite to the Tata Steel building across the road. The park is maintained by Tata Steel. From here one gets an excellent view of the vast expanse of Maidan area, the memorial, Vidyasagar Setu and the high rise buildings of Chowranghee area. This park, as the name suggests, dates back to the British period, and is part of the vast Maidan area. The other prarks, mentioned earlier, have been parceled out of the Victoria Memorial precincts, and are a post-independence phenomenon.

Occasionally I had a round of the Victoria Park grounds too. Unlike the other three parks, it has an entrance fee of Rs 4. It has vast grounds with huge ponds on three sides of the building and it requires more than an an hour's brisk walk to go round the sprawling compound. The marble structure of the memorial looks resplendent in the rays of the morning sun. Much of its original glory is intact. This park too, like the other three neighbouring parks, has its regular walkers.

While going to these parks, I used to pass by a cluster of buildings located at the end of AJC. Bose Road, just after it

Vidyasagar Setu, Kolkata

crosses Chowranghee Road. The very first building is Maidan Police Station followed by the office of Kolkota Traffic police. The signboard on the double-storied building of the latter read "South Traffic Guard, Kolkota Police". Like so many other landmarks of Calcutta, it had a ring of the British days. Another reminder of the British days was the double-storied vintage building of 'Calcutta Club, ' on the opposite side of the road, one of the oldest and most prestigious clubs in the city. Other buildings next to police offices, included Calcutta Information Centre, Nandan Theatre, Academy of Fine Arts and Rabindra Sadan etc. All these are hub of Calcutta's cultural life. Prominent posters are displayed on the compound walls near the main road, whenever there are programmes there. However films in Nandan, and exhibition of paintings in the halls of Information Cenrtre are a regular feature. Nandan is a favourite of people looking for old or off the track small budget films. The whole area comes alive in the evenings. I walked to the area many a evening to attend cultural programmes or see painting exhibitions of interest to me. My favourite were the music and cultural programmes in Rabindra Sadan. However, this was not the only place to which I walked to. I also walked to Aurobindo Bhawan at Shakespeare Sarani, and Gyan Manch in Pretoria St on a couple of occasions for attending the programmes. But I preferred to take a taxi to G.D. Birla Sabhagar. Weekend Planner of *Times of India* became my regular reference material.

Some of the most interesting programmes were part of Sharadotsava, preceding or during Durga Puja. One on Chaturthi in Rabindra Sadan was really good. It was named 'Mallar' but seemed unrelated to the Raga. It started with four or five songs on Durga, Odissi dance by several female and one male dancer, followed by a dance drama by a group of children all with quality performances.

Most of the programmes were in the evenings. The entry was invariably free, unlike Delhi where, excepting for some concerts which are held in open parks or exhibition ground, no programme is without a pass or ticket. And the passes there disappear with rare speed, with personal or subordinate staff or liveried chauffeurs in their shining limousines or white Ambassadors, having been sent with dispatch to collect them. It is a different matter that quite a few of them turn up to attend these programmes, more for being noticed as connoisseurs of classical music or cultivators of exotic taste, than for a genuine love of it. And for some others, the mere attendance provides material for small talk in some high end party or social get-together, or during the idle hours later on. These passes in Calcutta can be obtained without much fuss. One has to collect them within a reasonable time though. All the well-known venues in Calcutta are easily accessible by public transport, available till late hours in the evening. Metro station, tram and CSTC stops are at a walking distance from any such venue. And then the ubiquitous yellow and black taxies, a source of livelihood for so many from outside the state, are available everywhere almost twenty-four hours, rarely choosy, and ready to go even one kilometer distance and that too by the meter ! I remember my ordeal in Delhi when, on a few occasions. I did not have my own transport to attend these programmes in Kamani or Siri Fort, both a bit of isolated spots in the late hours. When the programme was over, I could get hold of a taxi or scooter only after walking good distance from the venue, and not without coughing up a substantially hiked fare. The meters of Taxi and autos just don't exist during odd hours in the capital of India. And one has to thank one's stars, everytime one reaches home safely. The two metros are thus studies in contrast. In Calcutta, it is the genuine love of music, and not one's means or social and financial standing, which determines who goes to attend these programmes. In Delhi, by and large it is one's means and social standing which determine it. In the former the audience represent a cross section of society, in the latter they are mostly elite, there however always being some exceptions on both sides. In the former, they could come in chauffeur or self-driven cars, or taxi or tram or bus or rikshaw or simply walk to the venue, and in the latter, almost always, by chauffeur or self driven cars. One cannot think of going to quality music concerts in Delhi by using public transport, without immense inconvenience and at one's own peril. Let us hope that the new metro makes some difference.

Sometimes I took an entirely different route, for doing my bit for the family, by way of replenishing the supply of fruits, vegetables and milk etc. This meant walking to Jadu Bazar on Ashutosh Mukherjee Marg, beyond the Elgin Road crossing. I located it by chance. One morning in the street, when I was still new to Calcutta, I inquired about the nearest vegetable and fruit market. As directed, I followed Justice Dwarkanath Road till it reached T-point near Khalsa School, turned right and after walking about hundred meters, at the meeting point of Ashutosh Mukkerjee Road, I reached Jadu Bazar on the right side of the road. As I was not happy about this route because of its congestion, I explored and found alternative routes to the market, reaching Ahutosh Mukherjee Road via Lala Lajpat Rai Road (even now popularly known by its former name–Elgin Road) or Suburban Hospital Road or Lee Road, which join it at a point from where it is called Chowranghee Road.

Jadu Bazar was a lively place, which comes to life from 6 a.m. onwards. It is a quadrangular building. Its double-storied façade facing Ashutosh Mukherjee Road, is about fify meters long. Single storied shops make the other three sides of the quadrangle. Inner side of the quadrangle could be approached through a couple of accesses from the front and two sides. Within the quadrangle there were lines of numerous elevated sheds with makeshift roofs. These were vegetable, fruit, flower, poultry, fish and meat shops etc.–the 'perishables' shop, so to say. The pucca shops in the quadrangle deal in groceries and durables. The market is a one point shopping centre with practically everything, medicines, cutlery, crockery, jewellery, clothes, electricals, stationery, hardware, kitchen items, pooja items—name anything required in an Indian house hold, and it is there, and at very competitive rates. It has a bank and a restaurant on its first floor. As the day advances, the place grows hectic. By evening and till the shutters are drawn, it is very crowded, with people jostling around. It is a mini India. It was always great fun to visit this market. It reminded me of my visits to Gadbadjhala at Aminabad during my student days at Lucknow.

One day I stood for sometime on the Ashutosh Mukherjee Road facing and studying this building. A cement engraving on the front wall gave the name of the market as "Jadu Babus Bazar." I suspect that the apostrophe comma, after 'Babu' may have fallen off, so that the word became queer sounding 'Babus'. The year of construction was not mentioned. But going by its design, it might have been constructed in late nineteenth or early twentieth century. Presently it was a municipal market, though originally constructed as a private market by 'Jadu Babus'. Like several other buildings in Ashutosh Mukherjee Road and nearby areas, it had high ceiling and high wooden venetian blinds, not in good repair, but had survived a hundred summers, such was the quality of wood in them.

Each region in India has some typical fruits and vegetables. Jadu Bazar displayed some fascinating variety of Bengal region, quite a few of which I had not seen before. My most memorable buy was fresh sweet corn pods. Two vendors regularly sold them in big round baskets on the pavement outside the market. When asked about the source of their fare, one of them told me that they came from Malda and Bardhaman, the other said that they came from Nadiad. But both said that American seeds were used for the crop. This corn was sweet and succulent and available round the year. They sold at Rs. 5 a piece! I had not tasted anything like this before. Then there were those two fruits, one called 'Rosogolla'which on peeling, gave a mild rose like smell, and the other, a smaller local version of litchi, round and smooth, sweeter but less juicy than the litchi of Muzaffarpur and Dehra Dun.

Whenever I walked into the inner market in the morning, I was invariably greeted, very gently, by words “Dada Asoon” or “Bade Baboo Asoon”. I was intrigued by the latter, but it did not take long to understand why I was addressed by those exalted expletives. Almost all the early buyers who came to that market, came in their chauffeur or self-driven cars, with a market labourer in tow, huge round basket on his head, to ferry the vegetables and fruits bought by ‘Bade Baboos’, to their cars. I too therefore earned the sobriquet of ‘Bade Babu’ under a mistaken identity, only because our entries to the market were around the same time. Though it was misdirected and a bit embarrassing for me to get this undeserved attention, I still enjoyed it. Mine was a moderate shopping for a small family. I could not be blamed if some of those vegetable and fruit sellers were discomfited with me later on. But I must say it to their credit, they never betrayed it, neither by their language nor their demeanor. I remained a ‘Bade Babu’.

One day while walking to the market from Justice Dwarakanath Road side, I noticed a big sweets shop. Its board read ‘Balram Mullick and Radharaman Mullick, Established 1885’. Attracted by its antiquity, I entered the shop. Apart from ‘Mishty Doi’, offered in earthen pots of different sizes, it also offered several variations of ‘Sandesh ’ and many other Bengali sweets, not seen in other shops. I bought some doi and sweets. While making payment at the counter, I saw a plastic placard on it which read: “Our philosophy is simple: We create perfection for those who appreciate perfection”. Everyone at home liked the sweets so much that thereafter, I always picked up something from it, whenever I went to that market. Having tasted their exotic products, I was convinced that the claim made by them was not after all, tall. I was not surprised when reading about the famous restaurants and cuisine of Calcutta, I found that Mullicks were mentioned as one of the best known sweet shops of Calcutta, with two more branches, one being in Park Street.

Majority of the buildings on both sides of Ashutosh Mukherjee Road are old and most of them are three or four storied. Date of construction in one of them was indicated as 1916. Many of them looked even older. Their high ceilings, ornate balconies with wrought iron or cement grills of different designs and ubiquitious venetian shutters, gave an instant and unmistakable impression that they were from a different age. And their struggle for survival was visible in their battered appearance. It is a matter of time before each one is replaced by multistoried structures of steel, cement and glass, like the plush Merlin, which has already come up on this road. High cost of maintenance, low returns and fabulous gains that modern structures promise, would ultimately wipe out these old buildings from the roads of Calcutta. The roads will remain but the buildings will keep on appearing and vanishing with the passage of time. The only building that will in all likelihood, survive and outlive all other structures of the city is Victoria Memorial. But its permanence too has to fit within a time frame of a millennium or two. Ultimately every thing gets sucked into the black hole of time. In the face of this impermanence the best bet is to prolong the life of these beautiful structures as much as possible. Science and modern technology would come handy in this effort. They have harnessed both very effectively in Paris, Vienna, and Rome.

The row of buildings on Bishop Lefroy Road and Suburban Hospital Road, where Shambhu Nath Hospital is located, always interested me, whenever I passed by them. The hospital is an early ninteenth century red brick structure of typical British design. It could as well have been in any English suburb. Other buildings namely, Chaudhury Mansion and polyclinic building, both opposite the hospital, are three-storied buildings in sound condition. The former is used as a residence and is well maintained. Then the four-storied building at the Chowranghee Road end is representative of many similar buildings in the area, partly dilapidated and crumbled, and partly occupied and well maintained. It has '64 Chowranghee, Restaurant and Lounge' on the ground floor. It seems to be a popular and upbeat place. On the Hospital road side of the building, there is a huge banyan tree, embedded on the boundary wall, and rising upto the second floor. Wooden staircases, from ground to top floor were visible on the side of the building, with apartments on both sides of them. Those occupied were well maintained, with modern glass windows and split air conditioners and those not occupied and abandoned were in bad shape. Small banyan and peepul trees, with octopus like roots clutching the walls at several places had caused cracks there.

Lefroy Road had several old buildings. And all of them, excepting the one near Chowranghee Road which was more like '64 Chowranghee' building, were in reasonably good condition. They were four storied, and like all other old buildings in the city, had high ceilings, some having wooden stairs from ground to top floors, on two sides and at least in one, on four sides of the building. Two had small domes on top and most had ornate balconies and big windows with venetian blinds. They were a mix of British-Saracenic architecture. The spacious apartments were being used both for office and residenctial purposes. These buildings must be a coveted address in Calcutta. Tata Tea has its head quarters in one of the buildings in the road.

When I had just started my walks after arriving at Calcutta, I was quite intrigued, by a group of shops in Chowranghee Road, near Lajpat Rai Sarani. They were 'Lakhy Babu's' gold and silver jewellery shops. There were several of them, mostly adjoining each other, and in a couple of cases, separated by one or two different shops. Opposite them on the other side of the road were two shops of well known P.C. Chandra Jewellers, which occupied the full ground floors of two old buildings. One day I counted the Lakhy Babu group of shops. They were fourteen in all. The common features and subtle differences in their sign boards were quite interesting. Let the common features be mentioned. These were the only shops perhaps in the entire area which had name boards in English and Hindi and only one had in Bengali too. Normal practice there was to have the boards in English and Bengali. All seemed to have some connection with 'Lakhy Babu ' or 'Laxminarayan'. Only one board had used the latter name, though. Perhaps 'Lakhy' was abridged version of Laxminarayan. Lakhy Babu in all likelihood, had founded the business in 1875, the date of establishment mentioned in one of the shops. All shops perhaps drew the bulk of their clientale from Hindi speaking Bihar and Jharkhand. The differences noticeable were mostly in the names of the shops: 'Lakhy Babu Ka Sona Chandi Ka Pahla Dukan' 'Lakhy Babu Ka Asli Sona Chandi Ka Dukan' 'Asli Lakhy Babu Ka Sona Chandi Ka Dotalla Dukan' (It was not clear if 'Asli ' i.e. pure or original, was meant to qualify Lakhy Babu or Sona Chandi). Only four shops had mentioned names of their owners, and all their surnames were different, viz. Sen, Sarkar, Dutta and Das. One shop had a photograph of the owner, which was more than life size, displayed by the side of its entrance. All were located on the ground floor of the buildings which appeared to be easily more than hundred years old. Most had old style round or square locks of enormous size and quaint designs, on their iron grills and wooden doors, meant to deter any prospective thief. Only a few had shutters. Once I found 'Asli Lakhy Babu Ka Sona Chandi Ka Dotalla Dukan' open early. Or maybe I was late that day for my morning walk. Someone was sweeping and cleaning the shop. I asked him how all 14 shops were using the word 'Lakhy'. He replied that all were one (Sob Ek Hi Hai, meaning thereby that they were all linked to a single family). His accent was Bengali. He was honest. The board in his shop had however made a different claim in as much as it said that it was the shop of 'asli' (the real) Lakhy Babu. When it came to doing the real business, the natural instinct of being one up against the rest got better of everyone and everyone claimed that he was the 'asli' or 'pehla' (the original or first) Lakhy Babu! The fact perhaps is that this jewellery business was originally started by one family, and as time passed, and families branched out, the shops of the families also multiplied, each claiming to be the 'Pehla' or 'Asli' one!

One day when I passed through the road during the day time, I noticed that almost all the 'Lakhy Babu' shops were having reasonably brisk business. The clients were separated from the shopowners or their staff by a thick iron grill. The manner of conducting their business had remained unchanged since the business was founded in 1872. And they have been able to hold their own against the likes of P.C. Chandra Jewellers, across the road.

The early morning walk to Jadu Market was not always pleasant. Often filth and garbage lay strewn on the road. But KMC (Kolkota Municipal Corporation) sweepers punctually hit the road around that time, sweeping and cleaning the roads and lanes. I wondered if this was a genuine sight of a city, that is more associated with strikes, bundhs, work to rule, chakka jam, go slows and trade unionism of every shade. I was in for a greater surprise one day, when it was pouring heavily for quite sometime since early morning in July. A KMC sweeper, lean and wiry, with only shorts on, swiftly moving, from one storm water inlet to another, removed the plastic bags and other material which were clogging them. This was in Bhawanipore area. I did not notice the type of heavy waterlogging there that one witnesses in New Delhi or Mumbai. Heavy downpours frequently cause chaos in these two cities. It must be said to the credit of Kolkata that waterlogging here is mostly over in a couple of hours. The sewerage system laid in British times, more than a hundred years back, seemed to be working effectively and that these very streets looked clean during the day, and gave altogether a different look in the neon lights later in the evening was to no mean extent, owing to the efforts of that lean and wiry sweeper and his ilk from KMC.

The pavements of Bhawanipore, particularly of Chowranghee Road, AJCBose Road, Elgin Road, Sarat Bose Road and Ashutosh Mukherjee Road, gave insight into another interesting facet of that city's life. This revolves round numerous tea, sattoo, juice, fast food stalls and eateries on the pavements. Everything, from snacks, beverages, tobacco products and equivalent of a meal is available here. While at Elgin Road, Lefroy Road and Chowranghee Road, they were at some distance from each other, they were in thick clusters near the gate of Nizam Palace and at AJC. Bose Road-Chowranghee Road crossing. In fact they made for a fascinating study in economics and sociology, unfolding an amazing saga of survival. The owners of these tiny establishments mostly hail from Bihar, Jharkhand, Orissa and West Bengal. Occasional exceptions are vendors from south, selling Idli, Vada and Dosa. And their small ventures, which require almost negligible capital, enable them not only to earn a square meal, but also to squeeze out a small sum to send to their cash-starved kin back home, cultivating a tiny piece of land or working as landless labour. The standard assets or capital or wherewithals, whatever one may call them, of a pavement eatery were a rectangular takht or a wooden box, some big alluminium utensils, a big gas stove or coke oven, a huge pitcher or big gerrycanes to store water, some stainless steel thalis, plates, kettle, disposable plastic glasses or kulhars, depending upon what one was cattering or vending. In some cases, there was tarpoline shed supported by bamboo sticks, for shelter in sun and rain. The list is illustrative and this could vary. For tea vendor, tobacconist, sattu seller, and Jhal Muree wala, wherewithals required and consequently the capital investment, including raw material cost, would be minimal, perhaps within Rs 1000.00 (one thousand).

By as early as 6 a.m. a passerby could smell the curries, steaming in the huge utensils, and see the pavement entrepreneurs kneading flour for chapattis, parathas or purees, or frying samosas or snacks. Clients started coming by 7 am and continued till late in the evening. The eateries mostly positioned themselves near the storm water inlets connected to the underground drainage system on the road, to facilitate drainage of used water and leftovers and washings of utensils etc. It was doubtful if they could meet the minimal standards of hygene and safety. But they did seem to address these concerns as much as possible in the given circumstances. What was however offered was, not only palatable, but also one of the cheapest in the country. It is unimaginable that one could, for istance, have a meal for as little as Rs. 10 which would normally consist of three or four chapaties, vegetable curry and a dal. And a non-vegetarian thali would cost Rs. 2 more. A Rosogola or any other sweet cost Rs. 2. Outlets near Nizam Palace gate and some other places offered many varieties of non-vegetarian and vegetarian food. It is a different matter that the food value or calories of these preparations could be negligible or near zero. Their value lay elsewhere. They helped to ward off hunger for thousands in Calcutta by offering a squire meal which was within their reach and, which, but for the low cost, most would otherwise miss. These eateries are a barrier against starvation. To thousands of eatery and stall owners, on the pavements of Calcutta, their tiny establishments mean ekeing out a living or bare subsistence so direly needed by each one of them. But they live, not at someone's mercy but out of the sweat of their brow. It enables both, those who provide this food and innumerable others who eat it, to scrape through life, just scrape through, from day-to-day. Thus in the city of Birlas and Goenkas these street entrepreneurs at the micro level hold their own!

The economy of these food outlets is amazing. Tea in a small plastic cup or in a kulhad (small earthen cup) costs Rs.

2 or Rs. 2.50, depending on whether it is plain or special, with ginger or cardamom. The quantity of tea in it is half of a normal tea cup in Gujrat, which itself is comparatively smaller than elsewhere in the country. The pint sized tea cups of Calcutta pavements had in fact given rise to a joke, which a friend there related to me. A burly Sardarjee from Patiala had once come on a visit to Calcutta. He stopped by a pavement tea stall and asked for tea. The stall keeper promptly poured tea in a kulhad and handed it to Sardarjee who gulped it in one go, and said, 'Cheeni theek hai, laa chai de' (sugar is alright, now give me tea). This tea was always freshly made and quite tasty. I had taken it on numerous occasions on my way back from morning walks. Made from freshly boiled milk, it was even better in the mornings. Some of these tea shops were so popular that people clustered around them from early morning. One such stall is opposite Haldiram's at AJC Bose Road –Chowranghee Road crossing. With sale price as low as Rs. 2 to 2.50 per cup, the profit on each cup could not have been more than ten or twenty paise. Ten or twenty paise coins have been out of circulation for quite some time. In Delhi, even 25 and 50 paise coins, though legal tender, are rejected contemptuously even by the vegetable vendors. In Calcutta, where profits from Rs. 10 food thali or Rs. 5 serving of Jhalmuri, may not exceed Re. 1 per serving, 25 and 50 paise coins are still legal tender and accepted freely! And for the economy of the pavement, where low cost services and items are churned out in large numbers and with unusual frequency, such coins are indispensable. Things might not work out to their advantage, if these vendors were to offer larger cups or bigger thalis at a slightly higher price. That might generate higher profits per serving, but numbers sold may fall dismally, thus making any marked increase in overall profits impossible. And tea is a special item in that city. For Kolkotans, being fond of taking tea frequently, the quantity served by the vendors in a Rs 2 cup is just the right one for them. Any increase in its prices, even

if matched by increased quantity, is bound to cut their clientale drastically. And the price and quantity being already at rock bottom, there is no scope of reducing either the price or the the quantity. This delicate balance, which suited both the buyer and seller, could not be disturbed without detriment to both, and therefore neither would be inclined for it! The economy of low cost and larger volumes, enables thousands of vendors in the streets to eke out a livelihood, just enough for keeping starvation at bay, and, remitting a small sum back home to keep the fire burning in the hearth there. These vendors would hate to have any mercy or pity shown to them. They worked under enormous hardships and earned little but with dignity.

On my visits to Jadu market, I saw how they slept on the pavement. Pavement was their home, in fact their whole existence. For bed, they had deflated card board boxes, hessian bags, plastic mats or sheets, folded tarpaulene, and worn out blankets, spread on the pavement. Occassionally one could notice a bamboo charpoy too. Vest and lungi or shorts was the usual dress for most. When I walked past them during my morning walks, most of them used to be sound asleep, some covering themselves with cotton sheet and some without it. The humming of flies, occasional mosquito bite, hissing of pressure cookers near by and the din of traffic on the road, made little difference to them.

And water, so vital for their existence, posed no problem for these pavement establishments, with KMC's oulets of free water available in every road and street of the city, giving plentiful supply. It was quite a sight for me one day when I passed through Burra Bazar and noticed water gushing out of a thick pipe jutting out of the ground in the footpath. There was a cluster of people around it, some with big containers or buckets, some washing their clothes and quite a few merrily taking their bath. Such abundance of water, particularly in a mega city was an extraordinary sight. I had not seen so much of water flowing so freely in any other city.

And it flowed back to where it came from—Hooghly. The river would remain an inexaustable source of water for millions, at least for the present and foreseeable future. Though untreated, this free supply is a boon for the city's masses. This may be unique in the whole world. Calcutta is paradise as far as water is concerned. Even the municipal supply to the houses through the taps is regular and for sufficiently long hours. The Nizam Palace complex, where I stayed, had water supply for twenty four hours. I had experienced this luxury in a residential area for the first time in my life in India. The slow pace of life of this city, which has so much to offer, therefore matters little.

Not every one was asleep in the pavement early in the morning. They had some sort of system by which some kept awake till late in the night to cater to the customers, while others went to sleep early. The early sleepers were the ones who were up early for the morning chores, busy cutting or cooking the vegetables, kneading flour, boiling potatos, preparing tea, or collecting water from nearby outlet. Their steps had spring in it. And there was something in their eyes that would clearly reject any patronizing or sympathizing gesture. The life was hard. But, having earned their bread the hard way, they lived with some sort of pride. And as one passed them, one was greeted by a strong smell, a mix of turmeric, garlic and coriander, emanating from huge and steaming alluminium utensils on the oven, where something used to cook.

There were two more factors which lessened the rigours of life for the pavement dwellers. The weather, being neither too hot nor cold, was benign. Rains were the only exception, and caused some inconvenience. The second factor was the easy availability of public toilet cum baths. The KMC and perhaps some NGOs have provided these in every street, not more than a kilometer away from any place. I had seen this in Bhawanipur. This must be true of the rest of the city too. The city was thoughtful and realized how essential these were.

They catered not only to the pavement dwellers, but to all, particularly the common man in the city. I peeped into a couple of them out of curiosity. It was remarkable that they were always manned, had regular water supply and were quite clean, all rarities in India. This is a paid facility. Mostly the charge was Rs. 2 per use. Urinal was free. And vim powder kept for washing hands in most of them, was on the house! But for bath, one had to carry one's towel and soap. No one minds paying this small sum. And these facilities seemed to have been around for a long time. No wonder the streets were cleaner and pavements livable in that city. This was a far cry from Delhi where, except for some posh markets or selected parks which of late have state of the art facilities, the public conveniences are in lamentable state, with most of them stinking, overflowing and choked. Even one visit to the interstate bus terminal or railway station is enough to prove this. It is nauseating even to go near them. People still go to them as they have no option. Absence of civic sense and adequate facilities, both are equally responsible for this. Overwhelming population is often cited as the reason for such a state, implicitly implying the impossibility of solving this and other civic problems. We seem to capitulate even before making an effort. In an age of advanced science and technology there is no problem which cannot be solved. If Calcutta can do it, others too can. The net result is that the public gets a raw deal even in relation to its basic needs. Some newspapers had carried reports sometime back that, Delhi is going to have about 300 'Seven Star' public conveniences in place before the Commonwealth Games. That was some consolation. However what should have come up long back out of concern for public or compunction for common man, to meet their basic needs, was coming belatedly, out of compulsions of the Commonwealth Games.

Calcutta does not forsake its pavement dwellers. It lets people live, unlike other mega cities which let its pavement dwellers wither away and die. It does not matter for this large hearted city, from where they come, from within or outside the state. Their being human is all that matters. The city of ageing buildings, roads and monuments has not allowed its ethos to die. It has something Indian about it. But as the time passes, the state will some day have to confront the unenviable task of reconciling two conflicting but vital tasks, viz cleaning and modernizing the city and its streets, without denying the pavement enterpreneurs of their livelihood. May be some relocation is the answer.

One of the familiar and interesting sights on the pavements of Bhawanipur, which isstill fresh in my mind, is that of a Hindi speaking 'Panditji', clad in dhoti and kurta, normally white, and doing his rounds in morning, thali in hand, which used to have some flowers, a small brass deity and a burning agarbatti on it. He would perform puja of the stall or the cooking area of the eatery or the oven, by moving his thali around them, and then put a tilak on the forehead of the owner. The owner then put a few coins on the thali, always readily and without grudge. Panditji was there punctually on Tuesdays and Saturdays. I am not sure about other days. Both, the stall owner and the Panditji, needed each other desperately to facilitate their none too easy existence. It was a symbiotic relationship. But while the stall keeper or the vendor could survive without 'Panditji ', the chances of survival of Panditji, without the stall keeper or the vendor were remote!

Once I was sipping tea from 'kulhad' the earthen cup, at a pavement stall. I preferred a kulhar because I thought it was more hygienic than the ceramic or plastic cup and it gave a wonderful earthy smell. As I was enjoying it, a few Bihari friends of the vender walked in and started chatting. One of them asked as to what was the date that day. Someone in the group said it was 27th. Someone else corrected him to say that it was 29th. One who had asked the date, turned to the first one and remonstrated with considerable relief and a smile on his face, "Arre Yaar, tum to hamara blood pressure bees degree ooper kar diye thhe". His friend had, at least for a moment, prolonged his desperate wait for the 1st! The tough life of Calcutta had failed to dim their witticism and sense of repartee, so typical of that part of the Hindi belt. Let there be just a straw to cling, and the zest for life refuses to die! And I enjoyed the lilt with which it was said, an inimitable lilt, typical of Hindi spoken in eastern U.P. and Bihar or the Bhojpuri belt, as the area is popularly known. I sensed the same lilt in it which, according to Chhanulal Mishra, an ardent admirer of Ustad Bismillah Khan, has crept into the inimitable 'tans' of Ustad's shehnai, thus setting them apart from all others. It reminded me of a popular number from a Hindi film of late fifties or early sixties, which started with the words "Khush hai jamana, Aaj pehali taarikh hai". The singer had sung it with abandon and feeling and captured the irrepressible joy of the pay day. It was a different matter that the euphoria of 1st was short lived and would evaporate, even before the first week was out and the interminable wait of more than three weeks till next 1st started again! The joy of 1st is still same for overwhelming number of people even today, at least in India. Certain things take long to change.

Sometime in March 2008, my grand-daughter joined a play school called 'Little Scholar' at Sarat Bose Road. It was at a walking distance from Nizam Palace. My daughter dropped her in the morning, and I used to pick her up around 11.30 a.m. every day. Sarat Bose Road is a busy road during office hours and traffic is very heavy. One day, on my way to the school, at the crossing adjacent to Indian Oil station, I saw a lady standing there, holding the hand of a 2-3 year old child, school bag slung on her back, waiting to cross the road. She could not cross it for about ten minutes. A tall traffic police man, with tooth brush moustache, in his white uniform and black helmet, was directing the traffic, with his back towards this lady. He turned after sometime and noticed this lady. He signaled all the traffic to stop, came to the lady, walked with the lady and the child to cross the road and then returned to the middle and resumed directing the traffic. I noticed this policeman at the same spot, through the whole of 2008. Their roasters perhaps took long to change. I will never forgret this considerate policeman's face. He seemed to be a natural fitment in the city with a soul, which cared for its women and children.

This errand of fetching my grand-daughter from the school was never dull. One of the days, when I reached the school early, I decided to walk a little further down Sarat Bose Road, upto Laxminarayan Temple. It has a small but neatly kept compound, with deities placed on an elevated and roofed platform. It was never without some devotees, paying obeisance to the deities. To the right of the entrance gate, there were office rooms, with two benches in front for visitors to sit, and a place earmarked for keeping the shoes. I liked the solitude of the place, right in the midst of a busy road and came there on many occasions later on. I spent the time sitting on one of the two benches. One day, on the wall behind the benches, I noticed a large sheet of white paper pasted on it, with something written boldly in black colour pencil. It was in Hindi, and read "Ganda Rajneeti se Mandir ko Bachao". From the manner of using the word 'Ganda', one could make a fair guess that the writer must be hailing, from Hindi belt, or to be precise, Bhojpuri belt, anywhere between Varanasi and Dhanbad. Further west the word, would have been 'Gandi'. The simple soul seemed to be genuinely troubled by a problem which was against his grain. The problem was politics in religion and religion in politics. If only he was aware that this phenomenon has bedevilled and shaken the whole world, including India, in the last couple of decades, and not that temple alone, his reaction would have been milder, closer to accepting the situation as an inevitable phenomenon. It was doubtful, if giving vent to his feelings in the shape of that appeal would have helped in resolving that knotty issue in the temple. One could not but empathise with him, even if one knew little about the actual issue which provoked that outburst!

My several visits to Calcutta during 2008-9 added up to nearly a year, each visit lasting between twenty days to two months at the maximum. And these several stays enabled me to see the city and a bit of the nearby countryside, through all the seasons of the year. The city and the countryside, unlike some states of the south, which have two or at the most three seasons, have four distinct seasons, much like the rest of Gangetic plain. And these have, through the ages, not only influenced but have got mirrored in its art, music, folk dances and festivals of the area.

When we first came to the city in November 2007, it was beginning of its winter, which, compared to Delhi, is mild and pleasant. It lasted till the end of February. Being a Delhiwala, I managed mostly with a shirt or T-shirt, except during the morning walks, when I put on a wind cheater. I however noticed people wearing wollens like half or full sleeves sweaters and jackets etc. During the nights, a bedsheet was my quilt.

With quite a few Anglo–Indian and Christian families settled there for generations, Christmas celebrations are an important part of city's life and add colour to its winters. The Park Circus, the localities nearby and their numerous churches, come alive with their large crosses of red paper and decorative lights during the night. And New Year eve in the Park Street is a rare experience, lively in a sedate way, but never as raucaus, noisy, and wild as new year eve at Cannaught Place, which often spins out of control.

The summer commenced early in March and lasted till May. It is hotter and harsher than Delhi because of the humidity. But breeze provides some relief all through the day, particularly in the mornings and evenings. The rains started in June. That time we landed on 1.7.08. It was overcast that day'and these conditions continued for over two weeks. In fact we saw the sun next only on 20.7.08, and that too briefly. It then disappeared again for several days. Typical daily pattern was a few heavy showers lasting for half an hour to one hour, followed by longer sessions of intermittent drizzle. Ocasionally the heavy showers would last for more than an hour or two. That invariably lead to waterlogging at numerous places for a couple of hours. This was the dreaded part of the city's rainy season. This pattern continued through August and part of September. Whenever there was depression near the state's coast, drizzles would be much longer and heavier, and strong breeze blew for a few days, all day and night, several times during the rainy season, turning the climate cool, sometimes even cooler than its winter.

Change is perceptible by the middle of September, as the rains are less frequent and taper off by the end of the month. Sun's appearances are more frequent and for longer durations, turning the days hot and humid again. It was Puja time, and the on set of autumn. And then came winter two months later. Occasional showers, mild heat during the day and some humidity continued through the winters also. In fact people mentioned that last year it had rained for almost eight months. There was a hint of climate change there. Delhi too is having its own version of climate change, with intermittant showers in May and June taking not only some of the sting out of the dreaded summer, but also the sweetness of its summer fruits.

Going Back into the History—a Visit to Chandranagar, the erstwhile French Enclave

Our first outing from Calcutta into the countryside was to Chandranagore in May 2008. I was keen to visit it for two reasons. Firstly, it was the only French Enclave in the north. And secondly, I wanted to generally compare and contrast it with Pondicherry and Karaikkal, which I had already seen, early in my career. Though about hundred kilometers apart, the two made up the French Enclave in the south, bigger and perhaps more important than Chandranagore. I had visited Pondicherry and Karaikkal easily more than twenty times, during my tenure as Asst Collector of Customs at Nagapattinam from 1971 to 1975. The customs establishments of Pondicherry and Karaikkal, too fell within the jurisdictionof Nagapattinam Division.

We left in a taxi around 6 p.m. We missed much of the countryside as it was already dark, when we left the city. Even though it is about sixty kilometers from Calcutta, via Durgapur highway, on the banks of Hooghly, it took us two and half hours to reach it. The stretch of road, after we left the highway, was narrow, and took nearly one and half hours to cover in the dark. We reached Chandranagore around 8.30 pm.

A friend had made arrangements for our stay at the guest house of an old jute mill, which was still functional. As we entered the mill through its iron gate, I could read the name of the mill: "Samnugger Jute Factory, Bhadresar". The group, as I learnt later, had another factory on the opposite side across Hoogly. The Samnugger factory had a big compound, with Hooghly forming one side of its boundary. Away from the gate and the manufacturing area and closer to the river, there was a residential complex for staff, some bungalows for senior managers and a double storied guest house. The latter was a French style building, with porch and garden in front and approached by a fairly long driveway. It had two large guest rooms, a lounge and dining hall on the ground floor and two large guest rooms on the first floor. The first floor was approachable by a flight of beautiful wooden staircase, having a gentle spiral. We stayed on the first floor. The room had high ceiling, spacious bathroom, big and high wooden doors and windows with wooden blinds and long brass latches, almost a meter long. There were huge teak beds, almost king sized, with high ornate back rest and legs. There were several windows on two sides of the room. Opening of even one window could flood the room with light and air in an instant. Between the two rooms of the first floor there was a large semicircular balcony with high windows and blinds, facing Hooghly about hundred meters away. Both the rooms had access to the balcony. It formed the frontage of the building. This was a nineteenth century French style vintage house.

Next morning, while the rest of the family was asleep, I set out after taking tea. The tranquility of the entire place seemed to greet me. I stepped into the lawn in front of the guest house. It was well maintained. As I walked on the soft green grass of the front lawn, cool with the morning dew, I had a long look at the guest house building, in the clear light of the morning. It was quite well kept for its age. Its design was simple but elegant. Leaving the lawn after sometime, I walked towards Hooghly and reached the private jetty of the factory on its banks. I stood there for a while, gazing in wonder at the mighty Hooghly, which was more than half a kilometer wide at that point. A carpet of green grass and some habitation thereafter was visible on the opposite bank. With so much of life and history along its path, this river, whose waters seemed inexhaustible, and which retained much of its purity till it merged with the ocean, had charmed me from my early days. The charm grew as the years went by and as I saw it in different stages of its journey at Hardwar, Allahabad, Varanasi, Patna and Kolkata. I walked upto the end of the jetty and dipped my forehand, into its waters to have its feel. It was soothingly cool, a sensation which is best expressed by the Hindi word 'Nirmal'. The words from the song sung by D.V. Paluskar flitted through my mind at that point, and the magic of that voice made me oblivious even of those sylvan surroundings for a few moments: "Chalo mana Ganga Jamuna teer; Ganga Jamuna nirmal paani". Its water was muddy, but not dirty. And I could not only see the flow of the river but even feel its current –a sign that the river, so far away from its snowy origins, was still alive, even at the concluding stages of its journey before it merged with sea. And it still had that jade like hue, though faint by now, with which it starts its its journey from the Himalayan snows, thousands of kilometers away. Jamuna in contrast dies a tragic death, at the prime of youth, its water almost stagnant and dark with pollution, soon after it emerges from the Himalayan foot hills, and before it reaches even Delhi. It is resuscitated for about three months during monsoon, to relapse into its now normal condition—a torpid, stinking and almost a dead river, which is finally redeemed at Allahabad by its bigger sister, but not without somewhat sullying its own waters, and threatrning its own survival. But Ganges, this mass of ice pure water, after emanating from Basudhara and Gomukh glacier in the Garhwal Himalayas, this 'Sursari', (river of gods) called so from ancient times, survives endless onslaughts of pollution all along its path, because of its sheer volume, ever augmented by numerous other Himalayan rivers, comparatively cleaner, both from India and Nepal, which keep on joining it, all along its route till almost the end. This capacity may not be inexhaustible, though one wishes it to be so for this divine river, the lifeline of the northern plains and sacred for the whole of India. It needs urgent attention.

A solitary launch belonging to the factory was tied by a rope to the jetty, mildly buffeted by the waves of the river, it gently moved from side to side, as if matching its steps in dance with the waves. The place had a quietness which seemed to gently press against one's senses. There was no other sound there, except the occasional chirping of birds from the cluster of trees, rustling of water, and whisper of leaves swayed by the gentle morning breeze. Leaving the spot, I strolled along Hooghly, in the factory compound for about forty-five minutes, and then returned back to the guest house. The family was awake by this time. We went to the large balcony and had several rounds of tea from a large tea pot, replenishing the hot water and tea leaves a number of times. My grand-daughter was ecstatic in these new surroundings and scampered about for good part of an hour that we were there.

Bath and breakfast over, we set out around 10.a.m. We

drove through the main road of the city which is about two kilometers long. It has shops on both sides. It reminded me of Karaikkal. It was a quiet city. Its streets were reasonably clean and had a mix of old and new style houses. Turning right at one crossing, and driving another half a kilometer, we reached the 'boulevard'–the most famous and beautiful historical part of the city. It is a stretch of about one and half kilometers along the bank of Hooghly. Well maintained parks between the boulevard and the river, with large shady trees, lawns, flowerbeds and plants. And facing the river, are benches embedded on the ground at some distance from each other, all antique pieces, which catch one's eyes. They have wrought iron frames, with legs ornately curved. They are functional yet beautiful and comfortable to sit. Being a Sunday, lot of local ladies lazed about in the boulevard and its parks and children played around. It reminded me of the boulevard at Pondicherry. The two were studies in contrast. The boulevard at Pondicherry, was along Bay of Bengal. Standing on the edge of the boulevard there, one could see the breakers a few meters away, emnating from the blue waters of Bay of Bengal and terminating on the sand in white froth. It has some old buildings including the secretariat, all well mainatained, on the boulevard. But piece de resistance are the round 'Doane' building and the light house, which is still functional, and not far from it, the circular park opposite Governor's Palace, and the palace itself, not very large but quite unique, with its vintage furniture, large mirrors in their heavy and ornate frames, beautiful balconies and staircases, all well preserved. The churches, some other structures including its unique railway station, and the residential buildings, some of them exceedingly graceful, all representing the French architecture of that era, and the numerous intersecting 'rues', are some distance away in the interior of the city. Pondicherry has a touch of Paris. It is is in a class of its own. At Chandranagore, almost its entire history seems to be concentrated on its boulevard. Everything in the former, being the main French establishment in India, was on a grander scale.

There were perhaps two or three ghats along the boulevard, with steps leading to the waters of Hooghly. Originally they might have served as wharves for French ships and boats. The best one was in front of Dupleix's Palace, earlier perhaps meant for the exclusive use of the French Governors. The notable buildings on the boulevard were, the court building—a single storied edifice with tall Roman pillars, established in 1878, Sacred Heart Church, with a touch of Notre Dame; Joseph's Convent, established in 1861, and Duplex's Palace, with pillars similar to court's. Most of the palace is now a museum, with a portion being used as "Institut de Chandernagor" (French Language Institute) Being Sunday I could not see the museum and the institute as they were closed. I wonder why these historical places cannot be kept open on public holidays. The convent was a revelation. A sister present in the school by chance, which was closed for Sunday, kindly permitted us to go around. Its modest entrance, a wooden door in the building facing the boulevard, belied the sprawling complex inside. The floors in the buildings were shining and the whole premises were spotlessly clean. It had a chapel and a prayer hall within the complex and a large playground. The entire premises of the convent were enclosed by high boundary walls.

Having seen the the main historical buildings, some from inside and most from outside, we sauntered back on the boulevard upto the taxi waiting at the other end. This time I had a proper look at the other bank of Hooghly. I could make out at least ten tall jute mill chimneys, some distance away from each other, silhouetted against the sky, covering the entire length of the bank, as far as the eye could see. These factories seemed to create an illusion of distant castles. The entire area seemed to be an important centre of jute industry. And right across, opposite the boulevard, was a big white jetty, with pillars forming three arched gates, and stone steps descending upto the water of the river. No one could miss it from this side.

During this walk on the boulevard, I was amused to note how the city was spelled in so many different ways. In Dupleix's palace it was spelled as 'Chandernagor', in the police station as 'Chandernagore', and many buildings and shops spelled it as 'Chandannagor', 'Chandannagore' or 'Chandranagar'.

We drove back to the factory guest house. Our visit to the boulevard area was like a journey back in time for over three hours. The French enclave had not lost its character entirely. It is still worth a visit and I enjoyed every bit of it.

We set out again at about 2.30 pm. for a water journey in the Hooghly, lasting about three hours. The launch tied at the factory's jetty, being then free, was made available to us. We got into the launch, and we were level with the surface of the river. The river seemed to have taken us in its lap gently. It was a dfferent feeling from what one gets from the height of its banks or from a higher level. From that distance the river inspires awe by its sheer size. As the launch moved gently, we were oblivious of the hundreds of feets of water beneath it. At that hour of the day there was little traffic in the river. Some fisherman's boat passed us at distance once in a while. This river, which has potential for efficient waterways, is underutilized, particularly outside Kolkata. Fishermen had spread nets extensively in the river. As we moved, our driver missed the floats of the nets at one place and the propeller of the launch got entangled with it. We luckily detected it. It still took half an hour for the fisherman to disengage the nets which had got slightly damaged in the process. We first headed against the current for about a kilometer, closer to the left bank. There was a jute factory there but not much of other habitation. Beyond the bank, was gently sloping land, covered with short green carpet like grass. Then turning the launch right and taking a u-turn, the driver took the launch to the other bank and further onwards to the white arched jetty, which we had seen from the boulevard in the morning. It was as beautiful from near as it was from afar. On alighting, we were taken to a temple some distance away from the ferry point. It is a small but well kept temple right on the banks of Hooghly. It was soothingly quiet there. We paid obeisance to the deities, took a round of the premises and came back to the launch. This time the launch proceeded down the river with the current for about an hour and we got a remarkable view of the city on the right and numerous castle like jute factories on the left bank. At some points, the river was almost two kilometers wide, its vast expanse oceanic in proportions. There was gentle breeze and peace all around with no sound except the chug of the launch engine, and the crackling of water, incessantly sliced by the axe like face of the launch, and then forming two lines which rushed to the opposite direction on two sides of the launch as it moved. Around 5.30 pm. we started returning as it was time to leave for Kolkata. The sun was close to the horizon, by now its large round shape clearly defined by an amber glow. As it touched the horizon, its amber turned into red, which was at its brightest as the sun slowly sank into the horizon. And in that process, lasting a few minutes, a million rays cascaded from its big round red core, painting the western sky in an amber incandescence. This sunset too was no different from any that preceded it or would follow it. Its basic elements were same. Its million details were different. A scene made up infinite variables can never replicate itself. It is same yet different every day. And that is how it has remained in my memory, a scene unique to that day and, different from all others.

It was getting dark as we reached the guest house. We left after having a much needed cup of tea. In the fading light and through half the route to Kolkata, we could get some view of the lush countryside, with its numerous ponds, rivers and waterways. It was 9 pm when we reached Nizam Palace.

All in all, it turned out to be a delightful trip.

Shantiniketan—a Cultural Retreat and Tarapeeth

In the second week of July, 2008, we decided to go to Shanti Niketan on a weekend by Shantiniketan Express, a very popular and convenient mode of transport to that destination. It was a hurried trip. The train left at 9 am and reached Shantiniketan at 12.30 pm I had in fact visited Shantiniketan some years back, while in service, and stayed for two days in the Vishwa Bharati Guest House which overlooks the house of Shri Amartya Sen, also in its campus. This time around, we had only half a day to have a look at Vishwa Bharati and then to go to Tara Peeth thereafter and return to Bolepur, even if it was late.

On arrival, we went to the Guest House in the Central Revenue Building. It is located on the outskirts of Bolepur city, surrounded by paddy fields. After a quick wash and meal, we drove straight to Shantiniketan. It started pouring as we reached the campus. As the vehicle could not be taken beyond a certain point, the nearest place which we could visit in the heavy rain was the museum. The rain and restrictions on visiting certain places in the university, curtailed our visit. One cannot get the real feel of Vishwa Bharati without moving on foot, and in leisurely manner, in the wooded environs of the campus, passing the spots where open-air classes are held and students gather for prayers and other programmes, the mud house where Tagore lived etc. The house was under repairs. As rain showed no signs of abating, we called off the visit, with a sense of regret, after about an hour and half in the campus, hoping to come again, on a sunny day in future, preferably during the period when the annual festival takes place, and Baul music is one of the attractions.

We decided instead to find some solace at Tara Peeth, some hundred odd kilometers away. We left around 3 pm. It rained all through the way. From the windows of our van, we got ample view of the monsoon in full flow, endless paddy fields covered with sheet of water, overflowing rivulets and numerous streams and canals. And then for the first time I had a view of the typical mud huts of Bengal villages. Many of them were double storied. Their tin roofs were Pagoda like, but curved inwards at the bottom. It was getting dark when we reached Tara Peeth after two and half hours of journey. The temple is located in midst of rich greenery. After parking the vehicle, we waded through the flooded approach road to the temple, about half a kilometer long. Despite the rain, large number of people had come for darshan. It took us some time, but we had good darshan—some consolation after drawing a blank at Shantiniketan. We left after about half an hour. This time it was a journey in the dark, with drizzle accompanying us all through. We reached Bolepur around 9 pm.

Next day we took Inter-city train for Kolkata at 8.15 am. In fact it came from Malda. As we reached the station half an hour earlier, it gave us some time to have a look at the surroundings. The station was a vibrant place, with a lot of tourists, in addition to the regular commuters. It is a favourate place for a quiet week end, a small town, which has all the goodness of countryside. The station was quite clean. Its old, single sotoried building, somewhat Ramakrishna Mission like, was painted in yellow, with a broad red line running across its length just below the roof. It gave a distinct look and identity.

Our return journey proved to be different and far more entertaining and lively than our onward journey. Vendors with tea, coffee, and snacks kept on coming endlessly till we almost reached Howrah. After about half an hour of departure from Bolepur, one musician slowly walked in. As he played his music, he stopped for a few minutes near every row of seats. His music was simple, basic and timeless: he played flute to the accompaniment of ghungroo tied to his feet, giving intermittent jingle with a mild tap of his feet. Such was his mastery of Ghungroo, that he could bring down the sound of bunch of ghungroos to a faint but distinct solo, a single ghungroo playing in sync with flute. Knowing little about the local tunes, I did not know if he was playing a folk song or some piece of Rabindra Sangeet. But it was a soulful music and I got completely lost in it. The musician had a beard and dishevelled hair. But he wore plain clothes. I wondered if he was a Derbeshi, that Sufi like clan, in the countryside of Bengal, who I was told, have an annual mela in Birbhum. This man had a spark in him. He played for his bread but played from his soul. Being a familiar sight, most of the passengers took no notice of him.

After about half an hour, another musician walked into our compartment. He was in saffron clothes—a long kurta and dhoti, long hair but no turban. He sang a Bengali song, with a heavy, slightly hoarse voice.which had some lilt and touch of 'riyaz' (practice). His accompaniment was a four stringed instrument, Sarod like, but slightly bigger than it. He played it so well that his singing, by no means ordinary, could not entirely match the richness and finesse of the stringed music. But overall, the effect was magical and for those few minutes it riveted my attention. I kept on wondering whether he could be a Baul, that group of mendicant musicians and singers in saffron clothes, who have a mystique of their own, who roam Bengal's countryside, and for whom all religions are same, though they owe allegiance to none, but preach universal brotherhood. But my doubts persisted as he did not have that familiar turban!

The performance of these two musicians were unforgettable. Though rain played spoilsport at Shantiniketan, the musicians did help to wipe out some of my disappoint. I must make it again to Shantiniketan, sometime in future. But the musicians may not be there again. Certainly not the same ones.

Durga Puja, when Calcutta Leaves Everything else Aside

Come October, and Kolkata starts preparing for its biggest festival—Durga Puja or 'Pujo'as it is spelled and pronounced there. Shasti, the day when the real festivities start in most of the pandals and localities fell on 5th of October. The work of erecting puja pandals had commenced early in September. It went on at a leisurely pace. By the end of September, countless pandals, big and small, in different shapes, each having some unique characteristic, came up in different parks and localities of the city. For each locality it was a matter of honour and pride to have its own pandal, and as per tradition, everyone contributed liberally within one's capacity. Celebrations are planned elaborately, with committies formed for the purpose, managing all the affairs meticulously. Fairs, melas, and sales are everywhere. A unique and lively atmosphere could be seen and felt in the air. Words cannot describe it. One has to experience it.

A week before Durga Puja, I happened to notice an ad of West Bengal Tourism Development Corporation in *Times of India,* announcing special Puja cruises on Hooghly, from Shasti to Ashtami, in the mornings and evenings respectively. As the programme of the Puja Committee of the residents of Nizam Palace was to start in the morning, I purchased four tickets for evening cruise. The cost was Rs. 600 each. An on board dinner was included in it.

The funds for the Nizam Palace residents'Puja celebrations came mostly from the contributions from the residents themselves, each one contributing a fixed amount depending upon the number of family members or their guests likely to attend the function. The parking space on the ground floor of the multi-storied flats in which we lived, was used by the resident's committee for our Puja celebrations. It had sufficiently large space, both covered and open, for such celebrations. The covered area was used for erecting a mandap and creating dining space with several rows of tables for community 'Bhog.' The open area was used for putting up a makeshift stage for cultural programmes and placing rows of chairs for the audience. As I was to learn later, the performers in almost all the cases were children from the flats in Nizam Palace. Everyone, performers and audience alike, participated with great élan.

Shasthi was the first day of celebrations in Nizam Palace, as perhaps it was in most parts of the city. The deities with Durga at the centre, had been established in the mandap. Typical Puja drums started beating from early morning. A little later in the morning, there was Chandi Path from Markandeya Purana. The priest recited the Sanskrit verse with energy, but not without a measured, rising and falling cadence, a fitting invocation for the goddess personifying 'Shakti'. Residents kept on coming and going throughout the morning, paying their obeisance to the deity. I spent nearly an hour near the pandal, sitting on a chair and intently listening to Chandi Path. It was absorbing and unique experience for me.

In the evening, four of us, my wife, daughter, grand-daughter and I left for Outram Ghat to join the 6 pm cruise. We reached the ghat at 5.45 pm. The concerned govt staff guided us to the steamer, as we walked the red carpeted passage. M.V. Sumangal was the name of the small steamer that was to take us on the cruise. It was decorated and well lit for the occasion and anchored on Hughly, close to the bank. There were cabins with seats in the lower deck. Some people preferred to sit there. Majority went to the upper deck–the more happening place during the cruise. Lot of chairs had been placed in rows there, facing a makeshift stage at the other end. It was a singing programme by young and budding artists, consisting mostly of Bengali songs and some Hindi and typical Durga Puja songs. The atmosphere was lively. My grand-daughter enjoyed every bit of it.

There were about hundred odd guests on board. The

majority, perhaps not being first timers, spent their time listening to the music. Some first timers like us drew our chairs nearer to the railing, or occasionally walked either to the open space in the front or rear of the steamer, to have the night view of Hooghly and the city along its banks. I had not seen anything like this before in India. The steamer first went up the river, in slow speed perhaps not more than five knots an hour, throughout. A gentle but mildly nippy breeze greeted us. The steamer first passed by the majestic Howrah station building, right on the river bank. It had been specially lit for the Puja. It was a dazzling spectacle, made brighter by the darkness of the evening. The grand structure, extensively lit and rising from the water, seemed to "burnish" it in gold. The steamer then moved towards the Howrah bridge, with its gradually changing geometric lines, shining like silver and, silhautted against the night sky. Proceeding further, it went a little beyond Belur Math, before commencing its return journey. The Math and the State Bank of India buildng, flooded by gentle light from the sides, which gave a gentle golden hue, were other memorable spectacles. The high light of the return journey was the dinner on the deck. Despite the constraint of space, it was efficiently organized for a gathering much larger for it. Everyone got to fill his plate without much scramble, and ate either near the railing or sitting by the few tables kept near the serving area. The food was tasty. The non-vegetarians however had better choices. The dinner was over well before we reached back Outram Ghat at 9 pm.

On return, I kept on wondering why the state, endowed by nature with an invaluable asset like Hooghly, could not organize more such cruises to places like Chandranagar, Murshidabad. Chinsura and may be other places and also harness its enormous potential in numerous other ways too. For us the trip was fabulous. One could not dream of a better deal for as little as Rs. 600.00 per head!

On the Saptami, there was Chandi Path during forenoon

in our Puja venue. The drummers beat their familiar patterns through the day, with usual breaks in between. We came down and spent an hour near the Mandap. There was cultural programme from 6.30 in the evening, mostly by children. It was well attended by the residents, as was the case on all subsequent days also. The programme was very interesting and truly eclectic, as actors and audience hailed from all parts of India, and participated heartily.

Then came Ashtami, the core of the festivities, the day for which the whole of Kolkata waits eagerly. Our foursome, set out to indulge in what is favourate of the Kolkatans, that day in particular and during most of the four day festivities– the 'pandal hopping'. We set out around 9.30 am. Most people preferred to do this in the evenings, when all the pandals were lit brilliantly. But we chose the day time as we wanted to cover as many pandals as possible. Slow traffic and milling crowds make it impossible to cover more than two pandals in the evenings, particularly in north Kolkata. And then one has to park the vehicle a kilometer or two away from the venue, and the queues are too long. But the queues move smoothly, no one trying to jump them the Delhi style, and the arrangements of Kolkata police are excellent.

We started with College Street and Bow Bazar pandals. They were big, temple like structures, covered with cream coloured cloth, which from a distance looked like neatly distempered walls. The pandal at College Street was located inside a park with a pond in the middle. Large sized deities had been established in its spacious stage. People gaped in admiration and awe on the rich dress, size and craftsmanship of the deities. Even though it was still morning, large number of people had already come to the the venue. The pandal at the College Street is one of the oldest in the city, and one of the most popular. Having come to the College Street, we decided to saunter past the Presidency College and David Hare School, adjacent to each other, both important landmarks in city's history. We could not go inside as both were closed for Puja holidays. We stopped by the arched gate of Presidency College for sometime and had a good look at it. Its name and year of establishment were prominently written. It was established in 1817! Both the buildings, that of school and college, have typical European design of that era, having three high stories, with arched varandas all along its length. They gave majestic touch to the buildings. Then we passed by the Theosophical Society building, its first and the oldest office in the country established in 1887. The area was full of Chandni Chowk-like buildings, perhaps much older, with their shuttered doors and windows, ornate balconies and façade full of grill work, typical of that era. Though old, they were mostly intact and not much ravaged by time. We were to see more of these buildings in Chitranjan Avenue. Tagore's Calcutta is still intact. His own ancestral house 'Thakur Bari' at Jora Sanko was not too far from here.

Our next stop was the pandal at Mohammad Ali Park. Its pandal was a domed structure suggestive of cosmos and the stellar formations. This year, I was told, many localities, including Mohammad Ali Park had 'Theme pandals'—an innovation for the celebrations, each adopting a different theme. But inside, all were traditional and unchanged, with familiar deities installed in all their splendour.

Having seen the two most famous pandals of north Kolkata, we proceeded to south Kolkata. There was not much traffic on the roads at this time of the day. During the four days of Durga Puja, slow moving traffic of Kolkota becomes dead slow in the evenings. Bose Pukur in Kasba was our next stop. It was different from others, as it had no pandal but a wood and bamboo structure, with a huge artificial tree, very leafy, installed in the enclosed courtyard, thus, giving it a rural look. We then visited several pandals in Garhiahat area. All were quite big and had attracted crowds from morning itself. All seemed very popular, and usually a must in the pandal hopper's list. Ek Dalia was a traditional pandal, with deities made of a silver coloured material, and mirrored walls a la 'Sheesh Mahal', giving it a dazzling effect. In Jodhpur Park, board had been used for its pandal, and the theme was Shiva. Triangular Park, taking its name from the shape of the park, was a traditional pandal. Next stop was Deshapriya Park. Here the pandal was in the shape of a hut, made of straw mats, located in a spacious park, with several facilities put together for the children, which included a mini rail, a giant-wheel, some merry-go-rounds etc. Children seemed to be having a great time. Maddox Square was the last and the largest of the pandals that we visited that day. The square where it was located was a vast ground. The deities were placed in a large rectangular hall with high ceilings, and several openings on its sides, for easy entry and exit. Chairs had been placed in the hall to sit and relax and to have the darshan of the deities from there itself, if someone so chose. The hall could easily take about one thousand people at a time. Its vast grounds had a shopping arcade, selling mostly household goods, and eateries to suit every budget and palate, all erected for the occasion.

The crowds which were initially thin, swelled considerably at noon. Whereever one moved, the festive atmosphere was palpable. People celebrated it with intensity, which never deteriorated to wildness and tumultuousness or crossed the limits of sobriety, as happens many a time on such occasions in some other places in the north. The festivities here had a subdued elegance. It was a celebration from heart, which got naturally reflected in the demeanour of the people and no one seemed to have an urge to give vent to it by wild or unruly gestures. One rarely hears of incidents of misbehaviour and molestation here on such occasions. People were elegantly dressed in sarees and dhoties, though it is not uncommon to see some of the young generation in salwar-kameez, jeans, kurta-pyjama, designer pants, shirts and T-shirts.

We returned to Nizam Palace at about 2 pm, just in time for Bhog of our society, which had just started. The 'Bhog' or community lunch or dinner as the case may be, is an integral part of Puja festivities. It weaves a sense of harmony and belonging amongst the members of the locality. Nearly all the residents of our flats had come down to join the feast, and this was going to be the pattern for lunch and dinner till Dashami. These meals, though not extravagant, were always wholesome and tasty, rounded off by a sweet dish, mostly a Bengali one. Each day there was a different fare. Organisers always tried to add some variety by including some dishes from different states at least once every day. But what is unforgettable for me is the taste of those Bengali dishes of the Bhog and that atmosphere which Puja festivities alone can conjure up.

Ever present every day during the function was Khushdil, the 'farash, ' of our multi-storied flats, responsible for cleaning and mopping up of those fifreen floors and sweeping the parking area and the small surrounding ground where children played every day round the year. He was about fifty-five, lean, tall, slightly balding and an amiable character. He got totally involved in making various arrangements for Puja festivities in our locality. He was a live wire and had inexhaustable energy, was omnipresent and ever busy and on the move, but never obtrusive, quietly going about numerous puja related chores, or serving tea during puja and cultural functions, or making arrangements for morning and evening Bhogs, without doubt a kingpin of the whole affair, an indispensable hand for our organizing committee. He remains an unforgettable and fascinating sight for me, moving briskly in his immaculate white shirt and coloured lungi, with checks. His long experience was invaluable. He had mentioned to me that he was associated with the Nizam Palace Puja festivities for the last seventeen years on the trot. And it seems that it never crossed either his or the resident's mind that he was a Muslim. Neither of them bothered about it. I always wondered, but could never resolve, whether the word 'Khushdil', represented the state of his own heart, or that of all others when they came in contact with him. It could perhaps apply equally to both! He fitted well in that motley crowd of residents, who, cutting across the lines of different caste, creeds and regions, participated heartily in the function. It was a miniature India in its own way.

Around 6 pm my daughter, grand-daughter and I walked upto Subhas Park, also known as Northern Park, about a kilometer away from our place, to see the Pandal there. This structure was a grand effort, both as regards its size and beauty, constructed as it was on a large area of the huge rectangular park. It was a temple like structure, in typical cream coloured cloth, with five spires, the middle one being taller than others and deities installed in each one. Shiva and Durga were in the middle one. It looked like a structure of gold, silhauted against the decorative lights of the park, something like 'Sonar Quila'. It had an outer wall, enclosing the main structure like a citadel. And there was an artificial moat between the wall and the temple structure. Lot of labour and cost might have gone into the making of this grand structure. To me this was the most elegant of the pandals which I saw in Kolkota. The to and fro walk to the park gave me an opportunity to have a look at the old style residential areas of south Kolkata, having rows of three or four storied houses with high ceilings, large wooden windows and doors with shutters, all well polished, spacious rooms and varandahs, all houses well spaced-out from each other, so that each had sun and air. There were some bungalows too. Many of the houses were having their own puja 'jhanki' on the ground floor. One of the unique features of these old residential areas, is the absence of service lane, which in India are invariably anything but clean. The result is that all the the streets, whether in front, back or sides of the houses, are very clean.

We came back around 8 pm, well in time for puja and the Bhog which followed. All were invited for that day's midnight puja, also an important one, when 108 'deeps' would be lit and 108 lotuses would be offered. And then there would be symbolic sacrifice for the goddess, of a gourd with a sickle. We came down briefly in the midnight for this puja. Large number of residents stayed longer. Dilkhush too was there.

We attended the puja for sometime in the morning on Mahanavami. Three of us, including my daughter and grand-daughter, decided to do some pandal hopping today also. We went to Park Circus park first. It being only 10.15 am in the morning, there were very few visitors at that time. The pandal was one of the biggest in the city. It had the advantage of the huge park, in which lot of shops, including some from far off places outside the state, had been set up on three sides, selling a variety of goods. It had a temple like structure made of split bamboo sticks and having a unique beauty of its own, both in the interior and exterior. It would be quite a sight in the decorative lights of the night. When we returned around noon to our venue at Nizam Palace, Sunderkand recitation was in progress and it went on till 'Bhog '. That day's Bhog had Punjabi touch.

In the evening as the twilight was giving way to the night, we went to Lake View Road. The area had several pandals in close proximity. We parked our car at some distance from pandals. There was exquisite lighting on residences on both sides of the approach to the pandals. And the pandals were a study in contrast, all beautiful in their distinct shapes and styles: there was one which looked like a white marble structure; another was a bamboo structure, with small cane basktets fixed all over its outer surface; and yet another had beautiful images of deities in bright silver filigree work, somewhat similar to those of Ek Dalia. Many make-shift eateries had come up in the area, offering a variety of vegetarian and non-vegetarian items at prices suiting every pocket and served in a clean environment. The crowds swelled as the night advanced. One could feel and breathe the festivity in the air, such as only Kolkata could conjure up. There was magic in it. Despite the large and surging crowds, the atmosphere was permeated by a serenity and elegance, a celebration which drew its inspiration from soul, where each one, irrespective of which strata of society he or she came from, instinctively and imperceptively lived upto the concept of 'Bhalo basi'. No wonder that a celebration on such a massive scale, is by and large free from any untoward incident. And the elegance is reflected as much in the demeanour as in the attire of the people—ladies gracefully draped in traditional cotton sarees and men in kurta and dhoties, folded to perfection.

After spending about an hour and half at Lake View Road area, we returned via Pudda Pukur pandal, not far from Nizam Palace, near Rajendra Prasad Road. It was erected in the middle of sufficiently large pond, approached through a small bridge. This itself was enough to set it apart from other pandals. The reflection of the lights on the water gave it a dazzling effect. It was a rare experience to see a pond or Pukur in the heart of the city. Kolkata perhaps is the only metropolis in India, which still has some of these waterbodies right in the heart of the city. Elsewhere, modernization has wiped them out.

By the time we returned to Nizam Palace, Dhunuchi dance was in progress in our pandal. The dance was followed by Bhog, very enjoyable as usual, with a couple of Marathi dishes thrown in for a change that day.

Next day was Mahadashami Puja, when the celebratations come to a grand finale. As I was to witness later in the evening on the banks of Hooghly, it was really grand, in the true sense of the word. We attended Mahadashami puja in our pandal for sometime in the morning followed by Aparajit Puja and Sindur Khela, before lunch. In this, married couples perform dance and offer arati to the deity by turns. Nearly all the couples present participated in it, no matter if the steps of some, particularly non-Bengalis, were a little awkward. But no one bothered. What mattered was participation. Bhog followed, and it had my favourite Bengali dishes: Khichri, Brinjal curry, a couple of other dishes, and the trade mark 'Kheer'.

After almost five days of intense festivity, it was time to give a fitting send-off to the deity. And while doing so, she is beseeched to come 'home' again next year, which she always does without fail. Thus the feeling of sadness at her departure is set off by the certainty of her return after a year. And the send-off is given by conveying her, to the tune of dance, music, ringing of bells and beating of drums, all the way to the banks of Hooghly and then affectionately immersing her.

The venue of immersion is 'Babu Ghat'—the people's ghat on the Hooghly, not far from the official Outram Ghat. In order to keep the crowds within manageable limits, every locality is given a specific time for immersion by the authorities in the afternoon of Dashami. Some do it even on the following day. The time allotted for Nizam Palace residents was 5 pm. Everyone was free to join the procession to Hooghly. A large number of residents—ladies, gents and children volunteered. My daughter and grand-daughter, both were game for it and joined. My grand-daughter was the youngest member of Nizam Palace entourage. Four open, light commercial trucks were engaged for the purpose. There was excitement and anticipation in the air. We left at 4 pm, the truck with the deity and some residents leading the way. Other trucks followed. We got into one of the trucks. Being a senior citizen, I was given the front seat, and my daughter and grand-daughter traveled standing on the open space in the rear of the truck, along with others. We moved slowly, the drums beating and the bells ringing all the way. The traffic on the roads was predominantly made up of similar trucks, big or small, from different localities, people on them waving happily as they passed by. We passed by Fort William on the way, and covered approximately 4 km distance upto the Ghat in about half an hour. I got the impression that we were given a particular spot to park our vehicles there. Having reached the particular spot, everyone got down, and the deity too was lowered from the truck, to be carried upto the ghat, after we got signal from the authorities to do so. Till then, everyone danced and sang around the deity with abandon. I was also pushed into it, and I did not resist it. I took my grand-daughter on my shoulders and danced for some time. She was delighted. And then others took over by turns, immensely, delighted to dance with the youngest member of our group on their shoulders. I would have thought several times before I took my 4 year-old grand-daughter to such an event, had it been any other city. But not here. Hundreds, perhaps a few thousand trucks had congregated in the area. There was magic in the atmosphere. A sea of humanity was there. I had witnessed similar scene only once earlier, years back, further up in the river, on the confluence of Jamuna and Ganga at Prayag, during Kumbh mela. I was young then. I yarn to go there again and get lost in that sea of humanity, gathered for that celebration of life and faith, unparalleled in the world. Some may call it blind faith. But not so for those millions who gather near that confluence, every twelve years, and whose forefathers had done the same at least for three millenniums before them. The celebration here is every year. But both represent the undying and unfading mystique of Indian festivities linked to a timeless river.

There were hundreds of groups dancing around their deities, and moving slowly towards the ghat, to immerse them at the appointed time. The shapes, sizes, postures, and decoration of the deities, and the garments they were draped in, were myriad. And despite the mammoth crowds, things moved with some method. That one never hears of any chaos or stampede or unruly situation, which possibility cannot be ruled out on such occasions in India, redounds to the credit as much of the people as the concerned authorities of Kolkata.

We too moved slowly towards the ghat. On reaching, we stood for sometime at the top of the stone steps leading upto the waters of Hooghly. So huge and thick was the crowd that not an inch of space was available, despite the spread of the steps being quite wide. Wave after wave of people came, waited for sometime, and then went down from one side, as others came up from the other, making way for them, so that there was no jostling or confusion near the water, a dangerous situation at that spot. When our turn came, we stepped down slowly, helped by the professionals to carry the deity upto the waterline. The immersion itself was a smooth affair, taking not more than a few minutes for each immersion. It could not be otherwise, considering that thousands of deities from all over Kolkata are immersed within a space of two days. Our deity, like others, was pushed by professionals, further into the waters of Hooghly by big bamboo poles, and once afloat, were pushed by the swimmers upto a point where there was strong current. Once there, they floated by themselves for a few minutes, and then disappeared into the bosom of the mighty river, large enough to receive, silently and gently, the unending numbers, including the largest ones, to their eternal abode.

It was dark when we strode back to our trucks after immersion. We were back at Nizam Palace after about one and half hour of our departure! We gathered in the compound below briefly before dispersing. With deities not there, one could feel the void, a sense almost of loss and regret.

We gathered again at 8.30 pm for the concluding function at our place–the short cultural programme, prize distribution and the community dinner, this time without deities drums and puja. It was over by about 10.30 pm. The week just past was an immensely enjoyable and busy week. All dispersed hoping that next year it will be no less so.

Back to where I Started—Tagore and Thakurbari

Tagore, like Gandhiji, is a familiar name for every child in India. It was so at least when I was a child. The reason for the poet's familiariy was *Jana Gana Mana.* This familiarity for me turned into enchantment, when once, during my matriculation days, I heard someone singing 'Tumi kemon kore gaan karo he guni, aami ouwaak rahi hoi shooni' (I hope I remember the lines correctly) in a cultural programme at Almora. The singer sang quite well. It was the beauty and sequence of those simple words that cast their spell on me then, and which has not waned since. And a little later, I heard a recording of 'Jodi tere dak shooni koi naa aashe, Tobe ekla chalo re'. These had then kindled a desire to read some of his works. I thereafter read his collection of stories, which included 'Kabuliwala, and a short novel whose name I do not remember now. And sometime during the years of my graduation, I read English translation of 'Geetanjali'. I enjoyed it, but not without being conscious that I was missing the beauty of original Bengali words. That can happen in any translation, but more so for Tagore's work. Translation played spoilsport, and somewhat dampened my enthusiasm. Whatever little I read of him, left a lasting impression and an awe of his multi-faceted genius. But to my regret, I could never really go whole hog, to his other major works, something which I still cherish to do someday.

My visit to Culcutta revived the fascination, dormant for long, that the poet had for me. Two things contributed to this. My year-long stay at Calcutta gave me first hand feeling how Tagore as a versatile writer was placed on a pedestal by the people there, way above others, an object of absolute reverence and awe. Secondly, Rabindra Sangeet had made him a cult figure in Bengal, cutting across every barrier. Everyone seemed to be fond of it. Its popularity was unbelievable. Contrary to what an outsider like me is inclined to think at first, it was not a style of singing, like Gharana singing, something which was evolved by the poet. As his autobiographical writings show, he seemed to be well versed in classical ragas and was fond of classical singers. He did not fiddle with that tradition. Rabindra Sangeet to my mind, is singing of his poetry, his songs, set to simple music. According to Wikipedia, Rabindra Sangeet "uses Indian classical music and traditional folk music as source". This, while throwing some light on the character of Rabindra Sangeet, falls short of defining it. But, while deriving from Hindustani classical music, it is distinct from it. In the former, the words or 'Bandish' as they are traditionally called, are but a medium for unfolding the beauty or 'Swaroop' of a Raga through Swars. Their role, though important, is subsidiary. That is why Ragas lend themselves as beautifully to instrumental as to vocal music. But that does not mean that these Bandishes are just a string of common words, conveying a common place sentiment or emotion, Their scintillating language and sublime sentiments are as good a poetry as any. For instance these Bandishes,

> *"Kaun albeli nar, paani bhare re,*
> *Haan ri haan jhama jhum."*

And

> *"Kinu bairon kan bhare,*
> *mora piya moso bolat nahin."*

have a beauty which is ageless. Many of them are credited to Adarang and Sadarang, the celebrated musicians in the court of eighteenth century Mughal Emperor Mohammad Shah 'Rangeele'. In Rabindra sangeet, *swar* is a medium for bringing out the beauty of every word, thought and sentiment of a poem. In this genre, beautiful poetry is made even more beautiful through singing and music. Rabindra Sangeet, may better be enjoyed than defined! And there is much to enjoy in it as its themes are popular and elemental e.g. 'Barshar Gaan', and the style of singing and accompanying music, is uncluttered and uncomplicated, appealing to all, elite and commoner alike. The poems adopt to music with ease. And yet, each singer could sing them in his own way, like Gharanas which evolve their subtle nuances in rendering the Ragas, without compromising their basic character. While these thoughts were going through my mind, I decided to read a biography of Tagore, and then, primed with basic information about the poet and his family, pay a visit to Thakur Bari at Jor Sanko, the ancestral house of the family. The more honerous task of reading his entire works could wait.

I looked for his biography in the library of India International Centre, during a short break at Delhi. I was surprised and a bit disappointed that this rich library had just one biography of Tagore. Or may be, there were more but I failed to locate them. I now regret that I should have tried for one in the long row of book-shops in the College Street. But this biography, though brief, turned out to be well researched and readable. I enjoyed it for the wealth of information about Tagore which was new to me. I wished it was more detailed. And to my disenchantment, it did not touch upon Rabindra Sangeet.

My perception of Tagore, like that of majority of Indians, is that of a literary giant, who was adept in every genre of writing, a great musian and painter, a humanitarian, truly a man of parts, who was deeply nationalistic, and who had forsaken his knighthood in potest against the killings in Jallianwala Bagh. One takes it for granted that his emergence as a cult figure dates back to early part of twentieth century or around the time he received Nobel prize. His emergence as a cult figure, however, seemed to be a post-Independence phenomenon, after people had taken a hard look at his life and works. While his literary and artistic credentials were undisputed in his lifetime, questions were raised about his nationalism. The criticism, according to the biographer, which came from the contemporary writers, was that he had not used the powerful literary tool to fight for country's Independence, and his works were thus idealistic, and far removed from reality.

More interesting for me was this fact mentioned in the book that his best creative years were when he looked after his family estates in East Bengal, from a house boat in Padma river. This ambience—a house boat for home, the Padma and the surrounding expanse of green paddy fields, right upto the horizon, could stir even an ordinary soul. But for a sensitive soul, a Thakur Bari denizen, steeped in its intellectual traditions, the result had to be extraordinary. And it was.

Tagore was deeply influenced by western humanism. And that perhaps slightly detracted from his nationalism. But that is not to say that he was not a nationalist. The aggressive nationalism of Pal and Das distressed him and he spoke against it. To quote the author "He believed that the stumbling blocks in India's future lay in social problems of the country such as caste system. If the goal of political freedom is pursued to the exclusion of all ills, India may become a sovereign state, but her social problems would continue to trouble her and obstruct the essential quest for moral and spiritual freedom, without which her political freedom would be difficult to sustain." Two of the greatest men of the era, he and Gandhiji, who had tremendous regard for each other, were thus fundamentally different in their approach. For Gandhiji, who was deeply distressed by the social evils like casteism and communalism and other problems like poverty etc., nationalism and India's Independence were the prime concern. An Independent India could deal more effectively, with age-old social problems too. But despite his total involvement in the freedom struggle, Gandhiji worked simultaneously for the eradication of social evils. He could not accept Tagore's criticism of nationalism, which for him, was not exclusive. India's freedom and adoption of a democratic constitution, both have played vital role in eradication of its social evils.

The success which has been achieved in this regard so far, would be unthinkable without freedom and without the constitution that we gave to ourselves after so much thought and deliberation. But these problems are far from over and we still have a long way to go. Both the great men were right!

One could even go a step further and say that, in the ultimate analysis, their goals too were not much different in essence, though their paths varied!

By November, the mild and pleasant winter of Calcutta had set in. Climatewise, Calcutta would now be at its best for about four months. November morning could not have been more pleasant, with a mild, heavenly breeze blowing. We decided to take metro and visit Thakur Bari and the Marble Palace near by. Three of us, my daughter, grand-daughter and I walked upto Rabindra Sadan station, about a kilometer away, and boarded the metro going towards Dum Dum. We took tickets for Rs. 8 each upto M.G. Road station and reached it in less than half an hour, less than half the time that road journey would have taken, and at a fraction of that cost. As we came up to the surface, we were in the heart of North Calcutta, the original Calcutta. The road here, which was a continuation of Chitranjan Avenue, was very broad, even by modern standards. There were large four or five storied buildings, all nineteenth century structures, complete with decorative balconies, large shuttered windows and doors, with small Pipal and Burgad trees entrenched on the walls, wherever they could get even a small crevice to insert their sturdy roots, and in the process invariably creating cracks on the walls. Theirs was a compulsive greenery of those old buildings, a part of it, which threatened the the whole, and yet looked beautiful. And on their sides and back were streets, with more old style houses, making up the residential areas of north Calcutta. We walked for ten minutes to reach Jor Sanko area, and then taking direction from local people, reached Marble Palace first. It was 10.15 am and its large gates had just been opened for the public. There were very few visitors at that time. As per the guide, the palace belonged to Mullicks, who were dealers in gold and were amongst the richest in Calcutta in pre-Independence days. The family still has large number of properties in Calcutta.

The palace is a double storied rectangular building of

considerable proportions, with tall Roman columns and court yard. It has about two dozen large hall-type rooms on its two floors, which must have been luxurious living rooms when occupied. Most of it was now used as a private and smaller version of a European museum, full of western and Chinese artefacts, replicas of Greek and Roman sculptures, Rennaissance and some modern oil paintings, intricately crafted giant Chinese vases, billiard table and Victorian furniture, all reflecting Mullicks' opulence. The high walled family temple on right side of the compound was very well maintained. And next to that was a sprawling zoo-cum-garden, with fountains and pathways and a variety of trees and shrubs, with thick under growth, indicating that it was not so well attended now. Despite decadence, it was interesting to go round it. The present generation of Mullicks lived in a portion of the palace at the back.

After spending about an hour in the palace, we walked to Thakur Bari, a mere ten minutes distance, passing through narrow streets, with rows of old style houses, two or three storied high, some with pillored façade, and typical old European-style high doors and windows with shutters. Most of the houses clearly showed signs of decay, some quite advanced. We entered Thakur Bari from the gate on the side of tram line. It is a three storied red brick building, almost of palatial proportions, with covered verandah all along in the front on the ground and first floors. It was a simple structure, with large compound, a few large trees, a variety of shrubs and flower beds and surrounded by high boundary walls. Apart from this ancestral house of Tagors, several multi-storied buildings which possibly came up in the compound subsequently, are all part of Rabindra Bharati University now, which also manages the complex. Two floors of the main building, the first and the second, which were the living quarters of the Tagore clan for over hundred years, had been made into a museum. The first floor was the core of the museum, containing Tagore memorabilia. The rooms were air conditioned, and the doors, windows and furniture had been maintained in their original condition and were well polished. There was nothing exrtravagant about anything, which reflected a sophisticated taste of a landed class, a royalty of sorts. It had large number of well lit and ventilated living and functional rooms, including a labour room, large kitchen and Indian style dining hall, with a number of low stone tables for several people to dine in Indian style, in sitting position with folded legs. Everything had a palatial feel, though never intended to be so by its former masters and occupants. Then there were halls in the building and areas in the compound, which used to be earmarked for functions, cultural and creative activities relating to art music and literature, all part of age old family tradition, a tradition of the denizens, whose demeanour reflected their different upbringing and who looked ahead of their times. The place must have come alive, on numerous such occasions, year after year, for more than a century. This place, in addition to Shantiniketan later on was the meeting place of the eminent writers, thinkers and who-is-who of that age, all important personages, who were shaping the history of the times. Raja Ramohan Rai, a close friend of Tagore's father must have been a regular visitor here. I was reminded of my visit to Yasnaya Polyana, more than ten years back, which, according to the memorilibia available there, was the meeting place of some of the greatest writers of that era. The atmosphere of Thakur Bari and Yasnaya seemed to have a striking resemblance. We spent about two hours in the museum. It was like a trance, with Rabindra Sangeet playing softly in the background, all the time. The entire place was very quiet, as we were the only visitors at that hour, and it was a closed day for the university. A huge board, displayed in one of the rooms gave yearwise deatils of Tagore's overseas journeys. It was quite a revelation for me. He was perhaps the most widely travelled Indian of his time. 'Bhraman' was an important part of the family tradition, integral to the process of family members' education and life's experience. That they travelled extensively across the country, even when means of travel were limited and cumbersome, was therefore not surprising. Japan was the most frequented destination, with which he had developed a special, almost a spiritual bond. He was well respected in the intellectual circles there, and had quite a few friends. And this special relationship has been kept alive by the Japanese Government by closely associating with the upkeep of this museum. One cannot miss the subtle but meticulous Japanese touch in its cleanliness, get-up and arrangement of the memorabilia.

As we were leaving, I was curious to find the year of construction of Thakurbari at Jor Sanko. There was no clue about it in the building. But as per the biography, it was built by his grandfather, 'Prince' Dwarakanath Tagore (1794-1846.) Rabindranath was born and brought up there. It can therefore be safely assumed that, it must have been built sometime between 1820 and 1840–easily more than 150 years back.

We reached home around 2.30 pm, the entire trip, taking approximately five hours in all.

A Peep into Calcutta's Cultural Life

Second week of November 2008, is memorable for one more experience.

I always scanned through the Calcuta edition of *Times of India*, as much for the news as for the various cultural activities going on in the city. Around the first week of November, the paper had carried a news that a programme 'Thumri Rang' had been organized by Sangeet Natak Academy, New Delhi from 13 to 16 November at G.D. Birla Sabhagar, and that the passes could be collected from a particular address given there. I had the passes collected with ease. I attended the programme on three days. Suchaita Gupta, Shanti Hiranand and Chhanulal Mishra gave their performance on 13th, Murad Bano, Subha Guha and Ajoy Ckakraborty on 15th and Mashqoor Ali and Girija Devi on 16th, the concluding day. The hall was full on all days. Two performances stood out from others for me viz. that of Ajoy Chakraborty and Girija Devi. Shree Chakraborty sang in Meera Malhar and Girija Devi her famous 'Purab ang'. And then some of the bandishes of Shri Mushqoor Ali were unheard of for me. Their wordings were beautiful. A city, and certainly its cognoscante, tuned to the magic of Rabindra Sangeet almost to an obsession, was equally receptive to Hindustani classical music and may be, even other genres. They not only turned up at the Sabhagar sufficiennly in advance to form long queus, but listened to the entire concert with rapt attention. Going to the hall itself, with its perfect acoustics, décor, seating arrangement and the stage, was a delightful experience. For me the hall ranks first amongst the concert halls of Delhi and Calcutta. Everything was so spic and span.

The hall forms the basement of the Birla mandir complex, right below the main spires of the temple, quite a unique concept that. I entered the hall through a gate of moderate size on the left side of the temple at the ground level, manned by the security guards who were permitting entry after verifying the invitation card, followed by frisking. And as I stepped inside, and went down a flight of polished stone stairs, to the the lobby at the level of the hall below, I was transported to a different ambience, the subdued elegance of the Sabhagar. No motives could be attributed to the capitalists for this Sabhagar, often faulted otherwise, not long ago, for the numerous ills, real or imagined, of the city and the state. The temple and the Sabhagar have enriched the city's cultural life over the years. They are a unique landmark of modern Kolkata. Some may find it to difficult to stomach the thought that capitalists too, at least some of them, can see beyond capital and profit and think of common good and welfare of society as a whole. These, contrary to what many might think, are not the preserve of any individual, party, institution or ideology.

I took a taxi from Nizam Palace to Sabhagar and back

every day. It was a hassle free journey. Return during late hours, cost between Rupeess fifty and sixty only. Going to a programme was never so easy for me.

On all three days, I selected the same seat, the corner one in the last but one row of the middle section of the hall, by the side of rectangular wooden pillar. From the rear of the hall upto the front seats, there was a gradient. The lower half of the sidewalls, parallel to the two side passages, was covered by wooden panels. The upper half had life sized busts of seven saints each on either side, mostly of medieval Bhaki movement. They gave an impression of being embossed on the ornate square frames, plastered on the wall. The material used was golden in colour, with shades of light black. They dazzled when the lights of the hall were on. I tried to figure out the saints from names written below the frames or from their profiles in my memory. I could read the name of Rai Das in the bust nearest to me and could make out Meerabai next to him, being the only lady and Kabeer from his cap and beard, a familiar picture etched in my mind since childhood. On my right side in the middle was Goswami Tulsidas in his familiar close fitting skull cap like head gear, and last but one on that side was Soor, with his Dante like cap covering his ears, both resembling the pictures appearing in the school anthologies of Hindi poetry. I could make a guess about others but was not certain. One bust looked like that of Chaitanya Mahaprabhu, from a distance and the other like Namdev. They were well known saints from different parts of the country. Their verses, easily adoptable both to raga based and simple music, conveyed a timeless message in the language of the masses. It was befitting that they were given a pride of place in that venue They in turn bestowed a distinct atmosphere and grandeur to the place, a presence so live and impressive. From their elevated position up in the wall, they were like presiding deities, silently overseeing and blessing every performance. The hall was honoured by their hallowed presence.

An Experience Called Dakshineshwar

As December came, we were completing a year in Calcutta. And it was time to go. My son-in-law Ashish had been elevated by his company and posted from Bangalore to Calcutta. The family had been united after more than a year. We decided to leave in January 2009. My grand-daughter was delighted by one and saddened by the other event. Two areas however, closely linked with the identity of Calcutta, still remained to be covered: Dakshineshwar Temple and Dalhousie Square.

One afternoon around 3 pm we left for Dakshineshwar by road. We wanted to be in the temple around sunset. It took about one and half hour to reach the place. The car had to be parked at some distance. After alighting, we walked through a market, about half a kilometer long, with most of shops on both sides selling Pooja material, interspersed by restaurants and other outlets selling different items. The market and the temple complex was buzzing with thousands of people, men and women, young and old alike. The atmosphere was lively. This is the familiar scene here every morning and evening, particularly the latter. The temple structure is of typical Bengal style, high and broad spires tapering off at the top, their four sides curving in to a conclave shape, defining its unique and beautiful silhaute against evening sky. The entire structure is painted in yellow. It has three parts: the main structure, which dominates the entire complex, where presiding deities are installed. The small room, where Shri Rama Krishna used to meditate and preach is part of it; a big pillared hall where the devotees sing kirtans; and a long rectangular structure opposite the main structure, opening out to the park on the other side, parallal to Hooghly with steps leading upto its waters. Those who came by boats could alight here. The open space between these structures was covered with marble, and could take thousands of people. We first joined a long queue here to have darshan of the deity. After the darshan, we went to see the room of the saint. It was not much crowded, as people were stopping there very briefly. We stayed there for about ten minutes and the image of the bearded saint came to my mind, clad in dhoti, sitting cross legged, with his wife, a saint in her own right, sitting by his side some distance away, and preaching the devotees, all ears to him. One could feel the presence of the saint there. Some might call it vibrations. And some others might try to dismiss it as a chimera of the onlooker's mind or an illusion Whatever it be, it cannot be dismissed easily, when it relates to someone like Swami Ramakrishna, who, as he told young Vivekanand, had seen the goddess face to face! Some people may laugh it off. The believers and the faithfuls experience same vibrations, in that first floor room of his greatest disciple at Belur, overlooking Hoogly, as also the room in Pondicherry Ashram, from which Sri Aurobindo did not stir out for forty years, meditating, and composing Savitri, Life Divine and much more and the spartan kutia at Sabarmati, where Gandhi ji lived his ideals and vision.

We went to the kirtan hall next. There was a large gathering there and a Bengali kirtan was in progress. Five or six main singers, men and women, were in the middle, and large number of others sat around them and sang with total involvement. Those not singing, listened intently, some with closed eyes. We also squatted in the hall for about half an hour, and listened. These kirtans, like Haveli Sangeet, have a distinct style of singing. They have rapid beats, accompanied by dholak and manjira. The effect is electrifying. I had heard the recordings of these kirtans earlier. But hearing them live there was altogether a different experience. My grand-daughter pulled me out of the hall after sometime. She ran around in the vast quadrangle, paved in marble, for quite sometime and then went to have darshan of the deities installed in the numeroous rooms of the rectangular building, facing the main temple. And then we went up to the steps of the ghats along Hooghly. A lot of people had thronged to the spot to witness the sunset. So indulgent to nature are the people of these parts, that they witness its myriad shades and hues with a silent passion. They lingered on there for quite sometime after the sunset, till the crimson in the western sky slowly turned into the grey of the twilight, announcing the arrival of another night. By now the evening lights of Howrah town across the vast expanse of the river were visible. They had a gentle and far away look. Once in a way, a steamer passed by slowly, its lights leaving a shimmering trail in the dark and tranquill waters, till it was out of sight.

This was the scenario at Dakhsineshwar round the year, festival without beginning or end, its magic and joy reflected in the faces of those milling crowds, who are drawn to it, day in and day out. I would always love t o be one of this crowd and be lost in obscurity, anytime and any day. This obscurity is a wonderful experience, sobering and elevating at the same time. In these fleeting moments, one becomes aware of one's smallness in the vastness of humanity, one's ignorance in the surrounding mysteries of nature, the more one tries to solve them, deeper they become.

Magnificent Buildings of the Raj Era

I had passed by some of the magnificent old buildings of Chowranghee and Dalhousie Square many times. But my idea of covering them by a day long and patient walk, spending a lot of time in their vicinity and having a closer look, somehow did not materialize. That remains a disappointment for me.

Dalhousie Square has a large number of these old buildings, mostly of solid stone and in the designs of Victorian era or earlier. The pride of place however goes to Writer's Building and Governor's residence. Other notable structure is High Court building. These structures are so solid, that, despite their faded look, they show no signs of decay. One cannot say the same of the numerous other buildings in the area. All these buildings reminded me of the better kept buildings in Fort and Fountain area of Mumbai or around Fort St George in Chennai, or even those at Westminster in London. Each has unique design and architecture. One can have some idea of the grandeur of these old buildings from the restoration of one such building by Oberoi Group at Chowranghee. It is now a magnificent hotel and a majestic sight, particularly in the evenings. While government can do its bit to restore its own buildings in the area, the private sector, like Oberois, can do lot more in reviving the old grandeur of the city. The thin veneer of decay in its buildings and roads, stately even by modern standards, is waiting to be removed. Once that happens, many areas, and certainly the vast area opposite the Great Maidan, with Park Street and many famous 'Saranis' in it could be amongst the best in the world, as they must have been during the Raj. Lala Lajpat Rai Sarani, still better known by its former name Elgin Road has got some face lift in recent years. The road and some of the rennovated buildings, with showrooms of some famous brands, get transformed in the evening lights.

Kolkata must not drive Calcutta to extinction. Both together can make a fabulous city.